WOMEN OF FAITH™
STUDY GUIDE SERIES

RECEIVING GOD'S LOVE

FOREWORD BY

PATSY CLAIRMONT

THOMAS NELSON
Since 1798

NASHVILLE   DALLAS   MEXICO CITY   RIO DE JANEIRO   BEIJING

✦ CONTENTS ✦

✦ FOREWORD ✦

I love valentines!

I think it's a leftover from my childhood when I would decorate a shoe box , put a slot in the top of the box, and then wait for my classmates to fill it. Gratefully, they did. Boys and girls would line up around the room and drop cards in each mailbox. Adorable cupids, bouquets of forget-me-nots, and chubby red hearts crowded the brightly colored greetings — greetings usually touting one's fondness for the recipient, asking the age old question, "Will you be my Valentine?"

I still have the first valentine my husband ever sent me when I was 15 and he was 16. And get this — I still have a valentine I made my dad when I was 10 years old. I know I may seem sappy, but there's just something about love. It makes the soul sing, the feet dance, and the heart celebrate!

This study is a Women of Faith® "valentine" designed with you in mind. We care about you and we can think of no better way to express our fondness than a study on the greatest love of all time — God's love. Divine love that is tender and sometimes tough — tough in the sense that it is not the mushy-gushy crush of a fickle child, but it's the steadfast, holy heart of a God who has manifested His love to us through Christ. Talk about a valentine! He sent us His Son that we might know of His holy affection for us — "for while we were yet sinners Christ died for us."

I don't know about you but I am a visual learner, which is probably why I enjoy valentines. I can hold, touch, display, and reread, each of them reminding me of the sender's feelings for me. Likewise, when I see a sample, a map, or a model from a lesson I'm far more likely to remember it, which is why I appreciate "Trinkets to Treasure" in each section of this study. The "trinkets" are physical visuals, which help tack the truths we study to our minds, so we don't forget.

Life is breakneck for most of us. Exhaustion is a constant complaint especially among us girls. We feel, at times, overworked and under appreciated. It's easy to run ourselves numb, so we need the tender jolts of love-notes to thaw our hearts, to cheer our dispositions, and to remind us what this life is really all about.

Girlfriends, you are of value. You matter and you are loved.

—Patsy Clairmont

✦ Introduction ✦

Have you ever meandered through the index of your hymnal and considered just how many hymns extol God's great love for us? "What Wondrous Love Is This?" "O the Deep, Deep Love of Jesus." "Jesus Loves Even Me." Consider for a moment what each of these song titles is saying, the messages they convey: "Love Divine, All Loves Excelling"—God's love for us exceeds any other love we might experience. "Jesus, Lover of My Soul"—we have a Savior who loves us for who we are on the inside. "O Perfect Love"—flawless, faultless, fervent, forever love. And look at some of the lines: "Amazing love, how can it be?" "I will sing of my Redeemer, and His wondrous love for me." "O, how He loves you and me." "Thy loving kindness is better than life." We sing them with familiarity, but do we consider the truth behind these lyrics?

God's love for us really is wondrous, perfect, deep, divine. In this study, we'll take the time to look at the key passages in our Bibles that talk about that love. We need to understand the precious nature of the love God holds out to us in order to receive it with our whole heart.

*"I've never quit loving you and never will.
Expect love, love, and more love!"*

Jeremiah 31:3 MSG

CHAPTER I

GOD IS LOVE

"GOD IS LOVE, AND ALL WHO LIVE IN LOVE LIVE IN GOD, AND GOD LIVES IN THEM."

1 John 4:16 NLT

Have you ever tasted a Krispy Kreme™ doughnut? I'd never even heard of them before moving to the South. Where I grew up, we called such things "raised glazed" doughnuts—just one more deep-fried pastry with a hole in the middle. But wherever Krispy Kreme™ doughnuts are sold, they have been elevated to the status of a cultural icon. For one thing, they are everywhere. Every gas station and grocery store has a Krispy Kreme™ doughnut case, its clear acrylic shelves lined with row upon row of glistening doughnuts. What's more, these little gems have become an experiential must for out-of-town guests. Tourists are escorted to the nearest Krispy Kreme™ repository as a matter of course. But while all Krispy Kreme™ doughnuts are

CLEARING ✦ THE ✦ COBWEBS

Is your hometown famous for anything—some landmark, special dish, or other claim to fame?

> *Let's enter into the love adventure of our lives and seek creative ways of telling our awesome God, "We love You! We thank You! We will live for You!"*
>
> Sheila Walsh

considered delicacies, nothing compares to the ones you get fresh from the source. You see, you can go to a Krispy Kreme™ doughnut shop, where they put a red neon light on to let passers-by know when they're frying. That way you can pop in and get a boxful of hot, fresh doughnuts. The glaze is still gooey and those doughnuts literally melt in your mouth. When that neon sign is lit, the line-up is amazing!

We're here together to study love. Now we can't really say that love is like doughnuts, but we can say that love is good. We see it everywhere. Love binds together parents and children, husbands and wives, sisters and brothers, grandparents and grandchildren, and the hearts of friends. But nothing compares to love that comes right from the Source. God's love is unparalleled—an experiential must!

1. God has many names in Scripture. What does Paul call Him in 2 Corinthians 13:11?

2. Yet calling our Heavenly Father the "God of Love" doesn't quite go far enough. What startling revelation does John make in 1 John 4:8?

3. When someone is especially known for some trait, we'll often say that if you looked that trait up in the dictionary, that person's picture would be there. Needless to say, if we looked up "love" in the dictionary, God's picture would be there. What do each of these verses tell us about God's love?

• Psalm 57:10

But anyone who does not love does not know God— for God is love.

1 John 4:8 NKJV

• Psalm 63:3

> *Love is right. It is the strongest of all human emotions. Love is the ultimate invitation to life.*
>
> Nicole Johnson

• Psalm 108:4

4. The wording in some of these psalms is wonderful, especially as you look at them in the various translations. See if you can match the words in praise of God's love with the passage in which it can be found.

____ Psalm 31:21 (NCV)   a. My God loves me, and He goes in front of me.

____ Psalm 36:5 (MSG)   b. Oh, God, my LORD, Your love is so great.

____ Psalm 59:10 (MSG)   c. God's love is the wonder of the world.

____ Psalm 69:16 (MSG)   d. Your love is eternal.

____ Psalm 109:21 (NLT)   e. I am the LORD, whose love is unfailing.

____ Psalm 138:8 (MSG)   f. God's love is meteoric.

____ Jeremiah 9:24 (NLT)   g. O Lord, Your unfailing love is wonderful.

*L*ove is difficult to define. It is one of those intangibles—something we cannot touch, taste, see, hear, or smell. Still, we do try. The dictionary defines love as an intense emotional attachment. For many of us, love is just that—a feeling we have—and feelings can be very hard to put into words. It doesn't simplify matters to define love by saying that God is love, because we can't really define Him either. But think about it for a minute. God says, "I am God. I am love. These are My people and I love them. How have I behaved towards those I love? See, this is what love expects, how love reacts, what love is willing to do. This is love." It may not help us to slap a nice, tidy definition on love, but it does help us to understand what love is supposed to look like.

5. So if you had to describe God's love, which of these words would you find a way to work into your definition?

❑ Great
❑ Short-lived
❑ Unconditional
❑ Fair-weather
❑ Amazing
❑ Temperamental
❑ Unchanging
❑ Stingy
❑ Lavish
❑ Steady

❑ Inconsistent
❑ Perpetual
❑ Unwavering
❑ Complete
❑ Deep
❑ Thriving
❑ Easy-come, Easy-go
❑ Faithful
❑ Tyrannical
❑ Abundant

> *The LORD has appeared of old to me, saying: "Yes, I have loved you with an everlasting love; Therefore with lovingkindness I have drawn you.*
>
> Jeremiah 31:3 NKJV

6. What is Paul's prayer for believers, according to Ephesians 3:18?

7. God is all about love. His love for us is vast, immeasurable, *huge*. Do any of you find that a little intimidating? Does the very big-ness of God's love seem overwhelming at times? Consider what Jeremiah 31:3 says about the love of the Lord.

8. The bigness of God's love is indeed coupled with the gentleness of it. What does Hosea 11:4 say God has done?

DIGGING DEEPER

This entire study focuses in on the love of God. We are highlighting this facet of His character and drawing encouragement from it. But we shouldn't rejoice over those passages of Scripture we love and ignore the ones we don't care to think on. As in every area of life, we must keep balance. In this case, we must always remember that while God is love, He is also just. Take a look at this verse. How are these people deceiving themselves?

You make God tired with all your talk. "How do we tire him out?" you ask. By saying, "God loves sinners and sin alike. God loves all." And also by saying, "Judgment? God's too nice to judge." —Malachi 2:17 MSG

PONDER & PRAY

This week, stretch your mind and heart a bit as you try to comprehend the bigness of God's love for you. Do you have a view of the ocean where you live? God's love is much more vast and deep! Do you have mountains to admire? God's love is higher than they are! Do you live in wide open places—"big sky country"? God's love stretches beyond those horizons! Are you blessed with a view of the night sky, with all its stars? The love of God for you is higher even than these! Take comfort and con-fidence in the unchanging faithfulness of God's love. Give thanks for the gentleness of God's love. Pray that you will be able to receive God's love, for that is just the thing your heart needs today.

TRINKETS TO TREASURE

At the close of every Women of Faith conference, women are asked to play a little game of pretend. Each conference guest is asked to imagine that a gift has been placed in her hands—one from each of the speakers—to serve as reminders of the different lessons shared. This study guide will carry on this tradition! At the close of each lesson, you will be presented with a small gift. Though imaginary, it will serve to remind you of the things you have learned. Think of it as a souvenir. Souvenirs are little trinkets we pick up on our journeys to remind us of where we have been. They keep us from forgetting the path we have traveled. Hide these little treasures in your heart, for as you ponder them, they will draw you closer to God.

TRINKET TO TREASURE

This week's trinket simply must be a doughnut—if you can manage a warm Krispy Kreme™ doughnut, all the better! The world is filled with love because God is love. God is the Source of love. We look to Him in order to understand what love is all about and what love should look like. Deep as it is, our love has its limits, but God's love is perfect, limitless, unparalleled. There's nothing else like it, and it is ours to receive.

CHAPTER 2

GOD SO LOVED

"FOR GOD SO LOVED THE WORLD THAT HE
GAVE HIS ONLY BEGOTTEN SON, THAT WHOEVER
BELIEVES IN HIM SHOULD NOT PERISH
BUT HAVE EVERLASTING LIFE."

John 3:16 NKJV

There are those who call the Bible the greatest love story ever told. Whenever I hear that, there's a little part of me that always responds by saying, "Huh?" I mean, come on. Genesis through Revelation hardly qualifies as a chick flick. We know what a love story is *supposed* to look like. There should be a beautiful woman, a handsome man, and some obstacle to their love. These are the inhabitants of cheap novels—elegantly coiffed ladies who swoon in the arms of muscle-bound men. These are the Prince Charmings and the damsels in distress. These are the makings of fairy tales, in which true love always triumphs. Love stories should feature romance, passion, fluttering hearts

CLEARING ✦ THE ✦ COBWEBS

What's your favorite genre of literature—biography, historical romance, fantasy, mystery, cookbook, or what?

and flowery speeches. How can we possibly describe the Scriptures as such a tale?

But let's take another look at that Bible, gals. There may not be flowery speeches and fluttering hearts, but there is undying devotion, faithfulness, and sacrifice. You don't have to look very far to find the damsel in distress. The heroine of the story has been deceived, carried away and made a slave. She's sometimes called the Beloved or the Bride. What's more, she's cherished by the Hero, who's determined to free her from her captivity. His quest leads Him down a difficult path, but He's willing to go to any length, even to die for the one He loves. She must wait for Him, and He's promised to return for her. Someday soon He will come, riding on a white stallion, to carry her away to the home He has prepared for her. Then, they'll live happily ever after.

> *It is right that we should desire to live in a world full of love. Our longings for happy endings are good. All of these hungers remind us that our hearts are homesick for a better world—a world that runs the way it's supposed to, a world not ruined by sin.*
>
> Nicole Johnson

1. Awwww! Don't you love happy endings! But we'd better start back at the beginning. The Bible says God loved us before we even knew about Him, kind of like a secret admirer. Fill in the blanks of this familiar passage.

"But God _____ His own _____ toward _____, in that while we were still _____, Christ _____ for us." —Romans 5:8 NKJV

2. Why would God do something like that? Why does Paul say He was willing to save us, according to Ephesians 2:4–7?

3. Let's take a look at two verses that will take your breath away. In 1 John 4:9, 10, what are the two things God did in order to show us His love?

> *God is interested in the tiniest things in the world. He cares about us and what we consider important. He gives us the desires of our hearts. He completes what He begins. He knows us by name.*
>
> Luci Swindoll

> *God speaks to us clearly. He means what He says. What He says He'll provide, we can count on that.*
>
> Luci Swindoll

4. How do we know that this sacrifice was a show of love? Scripture tells us so! What does Jesus tell us in John 15:13?

5. We know what real love is because Jesus modeled it for us. What does the beloved disciple tell us in 1 John 3:16?

*I*t's a game we played when we were too small to talk. Sitting on a parent's knee, with our hands wrapped around their fingers, we were asked, "Guess how much I love you?" Then they'd lift up our hands and stretch out our arms as far as they could reach and say, "This much!" It was the kind of play intended to get giggles out of us, but it also reinforced for us the fact that we were loved with a love that was "so big."

6. Probably the most famous passage of Scripture is John 3:16. Let's freshen it up a bit by comparing some of the various translations of it.

For God so loved the world that He gave His only begotten Son, that whoever believes in Him should not perish but have everlasting life (NKJV).

> *Being touched by God's extravagant grace ignites something within us that causes others to notice.*
>
> Patsy Clairmont

For God so loved the world that he gave his only Son, so that everyone who believes in him will not perish but have eternal life (NLT).

God loved the people of this world so much that he gave his only Son, so that everyone who has faith in him will have eternal life and never really die (CEV).

> Isn't it a comfort to know that God's love is never miserly, never punishing of our secret, doubt–plagued thoughts?
>
> Marilyn Meberg

For God so greatly loved and dearly prized the world that He [even] gave up His only begotten (unique) Son, so that whoever believes in (trusts in, clings to, relies on) Him shall not perish (come to destruction, be lost) but have eternal (everlasting) life (AMP).

This is how much God loved the world: He gave his Son, his one and only Son. And this is why: so that no one need be destroyed; by believing in him, anyone can have a whole and lasting life (MSG).

> *How does one find God? He is in our prayers guiding our words, He is in our songs as we worship Him, and He is filling our mouths when we comfort a friend or speak wisdom to someone who needs hope. Count your blessings. He is in them, too.*
>
> Patsy Clairmont

Have any of these versions helped you to see something new in this old favorite?

7. Jesus loved us enough to die for us. What did that love accomplish on our behalf, according to Revelation 1:5?

> *He has delivered us from the power of darkness and conveyed us into the kingdom of the Son of His Love.*
>
> Colossians 1:13 NKJV

8. What else does God's love do for us, according to Colossians 1:13?

9. Love is wonderful in its own right. But God's love for us comes with so many ramifications—and good ones at that. What's just one more benefit of God's great love for us according to 2 Thessalonians 2:16?

DIGGING DEEPER

Many prophecies describe Jesus as the coming Bridegroom and the church as the waiting bride. Bridal imagery is really quite popular! Take a look at these various Scriptures, each touching on a different facet of the bride's anticipation.

- Isaiah 61:10
- Jeremiah 2:32
- Isaiah 62:5
- Revelation 21:9

PONDER & PRAY

You're a bride, awaiting her Prince, her Bridegroom's coming. Are you ready for His return? No bride wants to head down the aisle without every hair in place, every fold of satin smoothed, every detail attended to. She primps and preens and plucks. There are facials, manicures, pedicures. But what do we do to prepare for Jesus' return for us? Are we ready—relaxed and radiant—or are we up to our elbows in other matters—distracted, disheveled and disobedient? This week, consider the lengths Jesus was willing to go to secure your love. Consider the state you were in when He found you. And consider ways in which you can prepare your heart for Christ's coming.

TRINKET TO TREASURE

This week, we have celebrated the "so great" love of God for us. It wasn't hindered by our ignorance of it, our ungratefulness for it, or our inability to return it. God's love found us when we didn't deserve it, but it came when we needed it most. This week's trinket is a small key. It can serve to remind you that Jesus came to earth in order to set you free—to rescue you from the slavery of sin. His love unlocked the bars, unlocked our heart, and opened up a whole new world for each of us.

✦ NOTES & PRAYER REQUESTS ✦

CHAPTER 3

CHOSEN

"YOU ARE MY SERVANT,
I HAVE CHOSEN YOU AND HAVE NOT CAST YOU AWAY."

Isaiah 41:9 NKJV

When I was what is now called a "tweener," my Mom decided it was time to re-do my bedroom. Now I had been in this room since I was just two years old, and I loved it. The carpet was deep purple shag and the wallpaper was scattered with big pink daisies and purple tulips. It was unique. It was perfect. The re-do started with carpet—a sculpted mauve. But best of all was the fact that I was going to get to choose my own wallpaper. I was thrilled. We brought home free snippets of different papers. We borrowed oversized sample books. We held up this piece and that piece against the wall to see how it would look. Every night, visions of cabbage roses and sweeping lilacs and

CLEARING ✦ THE ✦ COBWEBS

Remember the days when recess meant choosing up sides for a game of kickball? When were you usually chosen by one of the team captains—right away, somewhere in the middle, or at the very end?

> *As God's children, our lives unfold daily like pages in a book. Each circumstance is a different chapter. Each page is a new opportunity to live out God's plan for us.*
>
> Thelma Wells

violets and pansies danced through my head. But then I came home from school one day to find double rolls of wallpaper piled on the kitchen table. Mom had gotten tired of waiting for me to decide, and had found a bargain. The paper was white moiré sprigged with clusters of what were meant to be wildflowers but looked a whole lot like weeds to me. I was horrified. I hated it. It went up anyhow. It never occurred to me to accept my mother's choice with grace or gratefulness. I was enormously disappointed because I had wanted to choose for myself.

Being able to choose for ourselves is important to us. But even more vital is being chosen.

1. Being loved, along with everyone else, is nice, isn't it? Group hug! But you know, it's even better to realize that God knows us each by name, and that He chose us because He wanted us for His own. What did the psalmist say in Psalm 65:4?

2. God chose Israel for His own people. He made His covenant with them and gave them His commandments. In return, He promised to bless them. Fill in the blanks of these two verses about God's choosing:

Deuteronomy 7:7 — "The LORD did not _____ His _____ on you nor _____ you because you were more in _____ than any other people, for you were the _____ of all peoples" (NKJV).

Deuteronomy 10:15—"The LORD _____ only in your fathers, to _____ them; and He _____ their _____ after them, you _____ all peoples" (NKJV).

3. God was choosy. He chose times and places. He chose men and women—servants and leaders, patriarchs and prophets. Match up these chosen ones with the verses in which they appear.

___ 2 Samuel 6:21   a. God chose Jerusalem for His city.

___ 1 Kings 11:34   b. God chose Abram and gave him a new name.

___ 1 Kings 11:36   c. God chose David, taking him out of the sheepfolds.

___ 2 Chronicles 7:16   d. God chose David because he kept His commands.

___ Nehemiah 9:7   e. God chose Moses and Aaron.

___ Psalm 78:70   f. "The LORD chose me to be ruler over His people."

___ Psalm 105:26   g. Jesus chose twelve from the disciples to be apostles.

___ Psalm 132:13   h. The LORD has chosen Israel for His special treasure.

___ Psalm 135:4   i. The LORD has chosen Zion for His dwelling place.

___ Luke 6:13   j. God chose the temple and sanctified it.

4. What blessing is proclaimed in Psalm 33:12?

*M*ost of us have probably read *Charlotte's Web* by E. B. White, a literary staple of elementary education. In this story, a young girl named Fern rescues the runt from a litter of piglets and makes him her special pet. She names him Wilbur, and showers him with all the love a young girl can show. Wilbur flourishes under her attentions, and by the end of the book everyone agrees that he is "Some Pig."

Women have a soft place for runts. Their neediness tugs at our hearts, and brings out our God-given gifts of mercy, compassion, and lovingkindness. So we don't wonder why God chose "the least of all people" to be His own. He wanted them, and they needed Him. And they flourished because of the love that was showered down on them.

5. Now you're thinking, "Sure. That's great if you're Jewish, but none of those promises apply to me." Well, hold your horses and take a look at Ephesians 1:4. When did God choose you?

6. Who are you, according to 1 Peter 2:9, and whose praises do you sing?

7. Peter's description of God's people is quite majestic. Do you look at those words and say, "Who me?" You might look at some other sister in the Lord and say, "She's all that!" But we're too weak, too fallible to deserve such words. Nonsense! What does Paul remind us in 1 Corinthians 1:27?

> *But God has chosen the foolish things of the world to put to shame the wise, and God has chosen the weak things of the world to put to shame the things which are mighty.*
>
> 1 Corinthians 1:27 NKJV

> *I am not an afterthought. All God's love–inspired preplaning for each of us is not haphazard or impersonal. His timing may throw me or His sovereign plan may grieve me, but I am always sheltered in His sovereign hand.*
>
> Marilyn Meberg

8. God doesn't just choose us, He chooses us for a purpose.

• How does God describe Saul in Acts 9:15?

• What was Saul chosen for, according to Acts 22:14?

9. At the very end, those of us who are with Jesus are described as what, according to Revelation 17:14?

DIGGING DEEPER

There are many, many more verses in the Bible about God's chosen people. Let's focus in on some of the New Testament verses. Each contains another tidbit of information about God's choosing and those whom He chooses. How do they broaden your understanding of what it means to be chosen?

- Matthew 22:14
- 1 Corinthians 1:28
- 2 Thessalonians 2:13
- John 15:16
- John 15:19
- James 2:5

PONDER & PRAY

As you go through the coming days, ponder over the importance of choice. We women like to have choices. Just look at how many shades of lipstick there are in the cosmetics aisle. And why else would ice cream come in at least 31 flavors? We like to look over our options and do our own choosing. Lobbyists even insist that choice is a right. God chose us, to love and to save. What choices can we make, do we make, should we make? Pray for a heart eager to respond to God's love for us and willing to choose the things that would please our loving Father.

TRINKET TO TREASURE

We all love the luxury of choosing, but nothing compares to the wonder of being chosen. This week's trinket is the runt of the litter—a little piggy. He'll remind us that God chose us, not because we were so very desirable, but because we needed Him. His love, showered down on our hearts, is just the thing we needed to thrive, to grow, and to blossom. He chose us before time began for His own purposes. He chose us for His own, to love us.

✦ NOTES & PRAYER REQUESTS ✦

_____

_____

_____

_____

_____

_____

_____

CHAPTER 4

THIS I KNOW

"CHRIST'S LOVE IS GREATER THAN ANYONE CAN EVER KNOW, BUT I PRAY THAT YOU WILL BE ABLE TO KNOW THAT LOVE."

Ephesians 3:19 NCV

How do you know someone loves you? If a song can be trusted for the answer, we could turn to "It's in His Kiss," which hit the top ten back in 1964. It's familiarly known as the "Shoop Shoop Song," thanks to the memorable support provided by the backup singers.

CLEARING ✦ THE ✦ COBWEBS

Ever listened to *K.T.'s Groovin' Medleys?* On that CD, Kathi Troccoli adjusts some familiar hits into songs of worship. Have *you* ever taken a love song or a ballad and changed it around a little bit to make it apply to Jesus?

Does he love me, I wanna know.
How can I tell if he loves me so?

Is it in his eyes (oh no, you'll be deceived)
Is it in his sighs (oh no, he'll make believe)
If you wanna know if he loves you so,
It's in his kiss (that's where it is)

Is it in his face (oh no, that's just his charm)
In his one embrace (oh no, that's just his arm)
If you wanna know if he loves you so,
It's in his kiss (that's where it is)

How 'bout the way he acts (oh no that's not the way,
And you're not listening to all I say)
If you wanna know if he loves you so,
It's in his kiss (that's where it is)

Beloved, let us love one another, for love is of God; and everyone who loves is born of God and knows God. He who does not love does not know God, for God is love.

1 John 4:7, 8 NKJV

Come on ladies! Shoop, shoop, shoop, shoop . . . ! Okay, *maybe* that's the way you can tell if a young man is in love. But how can we know that God loves us? Again, we can turn to a song: "Jesus loves me this I know, For the Bible tells me so." It's a sweet refrain we've known since childhood. Simple, yet profoundly true. How can we tell if He loves us so? He's told us so.

1. We can be confident of God's love for us—of Jesus' love for us—because the Bible tells us He loves us.

- How are we to love one another, according to John 13:34?

> *Scripture is filled with encouragement for our faith because we are so vulnerable to doubt and fear when we feel overwhelmed by life.*
>
> Barbara Johnson

- According to Romans 8:37, victory is ours through Christ, who . . . what?

- According to Revelation 1:5, all praise should go to whom?

> *If we can acknowledge that what we see in the world is not all there is, we are strengthening our eyes of faith.*
>
> Nicole Johnson

2. Knowing means confidence, assurance, certainty. We know that we know that we know! But it's also good to remember that we don't know everything! What does Paul tell us in 1 Corinthians 13:12?

3. Let's think for a minute. We started with "Jesus loves me, this I know," but that's not the only thread we've woven our faith from. The Bible is filled with truths that we can *know* beyond a shadow of a doubt. Match a few of them up here.

___ Exodus 18:11	a. I know that after I die, I shall see God.
___ 2 Kings 5:15	b. I know that whatever God does, it'll be forever.
___ Job 19:25	c. I know there is no God except the God of Israel.
___ Job 19:26	d. I know that God can do everything.
___ Job 42:2	e. I know that the LORD is greater than all the gods.
___ Psalm 135:5	f. I know that God is gracious and slow to anger.
___ Ecclesiastes 3:14	g. I know that the LORD is great.
___ Jonah 4:2	h. I know that my Redeemer lives.

4. Paul's enthusiasm is contagious. What did he tell Timothy in 2 Timothy 1:12?

5. We can share Paul's certainty in Jesus' abilities. What can we be confident of, according to 2 Corinthians 5:8?

We have to stand in the complexity of all that God is working on, not just in the simple part we can see for ourselves.

Nicole Johnson

6. What is another aspect of God's love and care for us which lends Paul confidence, according to Philippians 1:6?

*I*t's a silly little tradition, but familiar enough. Picture a young lady, sitting on a green slope dotted with wild flowers. In her hand she holds a daisy, and she's slowly plucking the petals and scattering them on the ground. "He loves me, he loves me not, he loves me, he loves me not." Hardly a reliable method for determining another's affections, but the lovesick find comfort in any little good omen. Thankfully, with Jesus, we have no need to gauge His feelings by guesswork or little signs. His love for us is constant, and His declaration of love was clear.

7. What does Paul want us to know, according to Ephesians 3:19? Why is his hope for us paradoxical?

8. In Romans 8:38, Paul takes a look at the evidence of Christ's love in his life and says, "I am . . . what?"

For I am persuaded that neither death nor life, nor angels nor principalities nor powers, nor things present nor things to come, nor height nor depth, nor any other created thing, shall be able to separate us from the love of God which is in Christ Jesus our Lord.

Romans 8:38, 39 NKJV

> *When we, by ourselves, know who we are in Christ, when we have a strong personal relationship with Him, then we have so much to offer each other.*
>
> Sheila Walsh

9. We are assured of Christ's love for us. "Jesus loves me, this I know." This allows us to do what, according to Ephesians 5:2?

DIGGING DEEPER

Nobody likes to be told "I told you so!" At least, not when we've just made some small blunder. But we can take comfort in Jesus' "I told you so's" of Scripture. He repeated that little phrase quite often!

- Matthew 24:25
- John 3:12
- John 10:25
- John 14:29

- Mark 13:23
- John 9:27
- John 14:2
- John 16:4

PONDER & PRAY

God was not coy in His love for us. He declared it to all who would hear Him in no uncertain terms. This week, ponder through the verses we've explored so far about God's great love for us. What would happen to our confidence of that love if even one of these verses was missing from the Scriptures? Give thanks to God this week that He's been so forthright in communicating His love.

TRINKET TO TREASURE

This week's little token hearkens back to that little game of plucking flower petals. "He loves me, he loves me not." Your trinket is a daisy. Its sweet simplicity can serve as a reminder that we needn't wonder whether God loves us or not. We know He loves us because He's told us so. We can lean on the Scriptures, for they give us all the assurance we need that we are cherished by our Heavenly Father.

✦ NOTES & PRAYER REQUESTS ✦

CHAPTER 5

RESPONDING

"WE, THOUGH, ARE GOING TO LOVE—LOVE AND BE LOVED.
FIRST WE WERE LOVED, NOW WE LOVE. HE LOVED US FIRST."

1 John 4:19 MSG

onsider the moon. It has very little to recommend it—cold, dusty, and airless as it is. The moon's landscape is pockmarked by craters and is lifelessly gray. Among the celestial spheres, it is a mere pebble, responding to those with greater gravitational pull. The moon has no light of its own—flat, dark, unremarkable. If it were not for the sun, we'd never even notice it. But the sun is there, and the moon responds beautifully to its light. The dull, dusty surface is transformed, and we see a shimmering silvery disk in our sky. We admire the play of shadows across its surface, and trace the familiar rings of its craters with fascination. The night sky is filled with its gentle light.

CLEARING + THE + COBWEBS

Which came first, the chicken or the egg?

We're not so very different from the moon. When we were lost in sin, our hearts were dark and lifeless. Our prospects were filled with dusty rubble and pockmarked with pitfalls. We lived in the darkness of ignorance, with no expectations of change. But when the light of God's love washed over us, we were transformed. In response, we beamed back, and others could see the love of God clearly reflected.

1. God loves us, and we cannot help but respond to His love for us. What does 1 John 4:16 say our response is?

2. Just as the moon only glows because the light of the sun bathes its surface, we only love God because He loved us first. John, the beloved disciple, tells us so in 1 John 4:19 (NKJV):

"We _____ _____ because He _____ _____ us."

3. God loves all His creation, but not all respond to Him. What does Deuteronomy 30:20 encourage people to do?

4. Our church services are filled with praise choruses telling of our love for the Lord. But it's surprising how few times the Scriptures speak of our love for God. Mostly, they speak of God's love for us! But here's one, and it's not surprising that it's one of David's—Psalm 18:1. Write out this verse here.

> *Our family enjoys good gospel music. We have discovered that praising God in song lifts our spirits, clears our heads, and opens a place for the Holy Spirit to speak to us.*
>
> Thelma Wells

5. We are urged to love God, and not in a half-hearted way. How are we commanded to love the Lord according to Luke 10:27 and Joshua 22:5?

It's an old saying, a riddle of sorts, and a familiar enough question: "What came first, the chicken or the egg?" For many, this poses a real puzzler, because without eggs there would be no chicks, and without chickens there would be no eggs. It's difficult to separate the two.

The same could be said of God's love for us and our love for Him. It's difficult to separate the two. There we were, walking along, oblivious to God's very existence. But then we heard of Him, believed in Him, and loved Him. For us, that love was the beginning of a lifelong relationship. We loved God and He loved us. But which came first? John tells us that we could not have loved God if He hadn't loved us first. Whether we knew it at the time or not, our heart was responding to His.

6. We respond to God's love by loving Him back. And when we do so, our lives reflect that love.

• What was the prayer of the psalmist in Psalm 119:5?

• How did Paul urge Titus to live in Titus 2:1?

• What should everything we do reflect, according to Titus 2:7?

7. Love is not the only thing we can reflect. What does Paul compare us to in 2 Corinthians 3:18?

8. What encouragement does Paul offer in 1 Corinthians 8:3?

> *But we all, with unveiled face, beholding as in a mirror the glory of the Lord, are being transformed into the same image from glory to glory, just as by the Spirit of the Lord.*
>
> 2 Corinthians 3:18 NKJV

9. What is rather startling about our love for Jesus, according to 1 Peter 1:8?

DIGGING DEEPER

Our hearts respond to God's love and mercy in individual ways. God's love may be changeless, but our love for Him changes and deepens as we grow. Read Luke 7:40–47. What was the difference in the two individuals' responses to forgiveness? Why was the love of one stronger than the love of the other? Does this parable help you understand some of the basis for your own love for God?

PONDER & PRAY

This week, take the time to consider just how long you have been loved. God knew you when you were small. He knew you before you were born. He knew you before He'd even created the first man and woman. He knew you before time had begun. And all that time, He loved you! Thank God this week for this startling love, and ask that your life might reflect that love. Respond to God's love in the transformation of your heart.

TRINKET TO TREASURE

This week's trinket is a mirror, to remind us that the love in our hearts is a reflection of the love of God for us. Our heart responds to the heart of God. We love Him because He first loved us. His love transforms us in visible and invisible ways. Our love echoes His. Our lives reflect His place in our hearts.

CHAPTER 6

IF YOU LOVE ME

"IF YOU LOVE ME, KEEP MY COMMANDMENTS."

John 14:15 NKJV

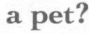

Don't you just love having plants around the house? There's something about a green and growing thing that seems to make a home homier! Now, there are two kinds of gals when it comes to keeping plants. There are those God has gifted with a green thumb. They were born to nurture and care for growing things. They've learned all about emulsions and fertilizers, soil composition and watering techniques. Always puttering over their plants, they're plucking, pruning, spritzing and singing. Under their care, orchids and ivies flourish and thrive. Their homes are verdant with lush foliage. Then there are those of us who are better off buying the kind of plants you have to dust

CLEARING
✦ THE ✦
COBWEBS

Why are children always told they need to prove that they are responsible enough before they can have a pet?

> *This is love, that we walk according to His commandments. This is the commandment, that as you have heard from the beginning, you should walk in it.*
>
> 2 John 1:6 NKJV

instead of water. Despite all our best intentions, plants wither under our touch. We over-water. We under-water. We forget to water. Leaves turn brown and drop to the floor. We have no idea what we did wrong, but every fern, African violet and philodendron that crossed our threshold wound up in the dumpster a few weeks later.

We may love having plants around the house, but love isn't enough for a plant to live on. They need simple things, like water, fertilizer and sunlight. And they need more complicated things, like dividing, repotting and pruning. You can't say you love your houseplant if you don't do the practical things loving your plant requires. That's a little like loving God. It starts out so simple. God loves me, and I love Him, so we can live happily ever after! But love comes with certain . . . obligations. Love isn't just a feeling. Love has very practical consequences in every life.

1. What does John say love should look like, according to 2 John 1:6?

2. John said this commandment has been heard since the very beginning, so let's go back to the Old Testament and the giving of the Law. What did Moses tell the people they must do?

Deuteronomy 10:12 — "What does the LORD your God _____ of you, but to _____ the LORD your God, to _____ in all His _____ and to _____ Him, to _____ the LORD your God with all your _____ and with all your _____" (NKJV).

Deuteronomy 11:1 — "Therefore you shall _____ the LORD your God, and _____ His _____, His _____, His _____, and His _____ always" (NKJV).

Deuteronomy 11:13 — "_____ _____ My commandments which I command you today, to _____ the LORD your God and _____ Him with all your _____ and with all your _____" (NKJV).

3. There are different ways to say it: "Walk the talk." "Put your money where your mouth is." "Practice what you preach." How does 1 John 3:18 put it?

You don't have to pretend with God. Risk being absolutely honest. Wrestle with your faith. Live your life authentically, always remembering that you are loved forever.

Sheila Walsh

> *It's easy to lose joy in life. We get to the stage where we take ourselves too seriously or are afraid to make mistakes. But when we know that we are loved by God, loved beyond measure, we can dive in and take a chance.*
>
> Sheila Walsh

4. Read John 14:21–23. What is Jesus' expectation for those who love Him, according to verse 21? And then, in verse 23, what is the promise made to those who truly love Him?

Now this may seem a little strange. After all, we just got done saying that God is love and God loves all of us unconditionally. All this talk about keeping commandments and doing good deeds smacks of conditions! We like to know that God loves us—it makes us feel good. We'd just as soon take that promise and rest on it. But remember, God loves because He is God. He shows the same mercy, grace and kindness to all. "For He is kind to the unthankful and evil" (Luke 6:35 NKJV). We *don't* need to earn God's love. He couldn't love us any more or any less than He does now. But what we're talking about here is *our* love for God. We believers claim to love Jesus. But how do we show that love? Is it just warm fuzzy feelings about our Creator? I should say not. We say we love God. But how do we return His great love? Simple. We live to please Him. We do as He asks of us. We obey Him.

5. First John 5:2, 3 has much the same message as the other verses we've looked at so far today. But what note of encouragement is tacked onto the end?

6. Paul makes an interesting request in 2 Corinthians 8:24. What is it?

> *By this we know that we love the children of God, when we love God and keep His commandments. For this is the love of God, that we keep His commandments. And His commandments are not burdensome.*
>
> 1 John 5:2, 3 NKJV

> *I have learned that pain has purpose, which, at the peak of excruciating discomfort, brings me little consolation. Hindsight, though, has often proven pain's value. In fact, I have found pain to be one of life's most effective teachers. It gains one's full attention. It takes lessons down to the bottom line.*
>
> Patsy Clairmont

7. Now there's no denying that obedience doesn't always come easy. We all undergo testing, trials and temptations. These are opportunities for us to prove the steadfastness of our love. What does James tell us along these lines in James 1:12?

8. What attitude did Paul have, which helped him to live out his love for Jesus?

"I have been _____ with Christ; it is _____ _____ I who _____, but Christ _____ _____ in me; and the _____ which I now _____ in the _____ I live by _____ in the Son of God, who _____ me and _____ Himself for me."—Galatians 2:20 NKJV

DIGGING DEEPER

God calls for His people to obey the commands He gave to them. These were not hardships, and often carried with them the promise of blessings when obeyed.

- Psalm 103:17, 18
- John 15:10

PONDER & PRAY

Love has its intentional side. Our actions demonstrate the love we carry in our hearts. They're the proof, the evidence, the verification of what we claim. This week, pray for the eyes to see the practical side of love. In your relationships with people and your relationship with God, take note of the things we do because of our love. Make a conscious effort to excel in demonstrating your love in tangible ways.

TRINKET TO TREASURE

This week we compared our love for God with our love for houseplants. Just as we cannot expect a plant to survive without taking care of its practical needs, we must accept that there are practical consequences to loving the Lord. So this week's trinket is a plant mister. A houseplant needs constant nurturing in order to grow and mature. Our love for God, in order for it to mature, must be accompanied by obedience. "If you love Me, you'll keep my command-ments."

✦ NOTES & PRAYER REQUESTS ✦

CHAPTER 7

SET YOUR AFFECTIONS

"SET YOUR MIND ON THINGS ABOVE,
NOT ON THINGS ON THE EARTH."

Colossians 3:2 NKJV

Hairstyles go in and out of style. Sometimes the look is sleek and shiny. Sometimes it's a sporty wash-n-wear look. There've been shags and pageboys, twists and flips, Afros and cornrows. There are French twists and French braids. Poodle perms and ponytails. Beehives, bouffants, baby bangs and buns. But no matter the current rage, there are always those of us who wish our hair had a little more bounce. We long for curls!

Now there are a lot of ways to get curls, and most involve some version of the curler. There are hot rollers and sponge rollers. There are bristly rollers that are just awful to sleep on. Then you've got

CLEARING ✦ THE ✦ COBWEBS

Do you have any pictures of yourself that are embarrassing to you now because of the way you were styling your hair at the time they were taken?

> *Every day we must renew our minds. I don't think God means do not plan, do not look forward to days to come. I believe He means that right now is the only opportunity we have to live for Him*
>
> Thelma Wells

your pin curls and your rag curls. There are perm rods and pink snappies. Some of us like the crimped look of hair that's been braided, then brushed out. But no matter what method you use, the concept is the same. The hair is wrapped around the curler. With time (and perhaps a little heat), the hair begins to change its ways. Instead of being its old straight self, it conforms itself to the shape of the curler. When the time comes to unwind, your hair has a whole new look. Spirals, ringlets, soft waves—curls!

Well, we need to set more than our hair. We need to set our hearts!

1. Psalm 78:8 gives us an example of those who have their hearts set, but not properly.

"And may not be like their fathers, A _____ and _____ generation, A generation that did not _____ its _____ _____, And whose _____ was not _____ to God."—Psalm 78:8 NKJV

2. If we are to set our heart aright, we mustn't follow the example of those "whose end is destruction, whose god is their belly, and whose glory is in their shame—who set their mind on earthly things" (Phil. 3:19 NKJV).

- Solomon insists that ignorance is not bliss. What do the simple love in Proverbs 1:22?

- Ezekiel doesn't hold with those whose walk doesn't match their talk. What do the people in Ezekiel 33:31 have their hearts set on?

- Jesus berated those who liked to impress others with their religious fervor. What do the hypocrites love according to Matthew 6:5?

- Dressing up in your finest clothes and trading the latest gossip won't endear you to the Father. What does Mark 12:38 warn us against?

- There cannot be real love where people wear masks. What does Paul say can have no part in our love for one another?

3. We like to have positive role-models-mentors. And Scripture is filled with positive instruction—"do this," "pursue this," "choose this." But we can learn just as much from Scripture's negative examples if we are teachable. These verses warn us from setting our affections on the wrong things. Match up these below.

___ Psalm 4:2   a. Do not love the best places and best seats.

___ Psalm 62:10   b. Do not love to wander on unrestrained feet.

___ Proverbs 17:19   c. Do not love this present world.

___ Proverbs 20:13   d. Do not love transgression.

___ Ecclesiastes 5:10   e. Do not love oppression.

___ Jeremiah 14:10   f. Do not love sleep.

___ Hosea 12:7   g. Do not love the praise of men.

___ Zechariah 8:17   h. Do not set your heart on riches.

___ Matthew 23:6   i. Do not love the world and the things of the world.

___ John 12:43   j. Do not love worthlessness or seek falsehood.

___ 1 Timothy 6:10   k. Do not love a false oath.

___ 2 Timothy 4:10   l. Do not love silver, for it will not satisfy.

___ 1 John 2:15   m. Do not love money, it is the root of all evil.

4. So what should we set our hearts on according to Deuteronomy 32:46?

5. What does the first part of 1 Chronicles 22:19 urge Solomon to do?

> *Now set your heart and your soul to seek the LORD your God.*
>
> 1 Chronicles 22:19a NKJV

ave you ever noticed that once you've set your hair, you have to be very careful with it in order to maintain the set? We're talking heavy-duty hair spray. You'll need scarves for windy days. Don't even think about riding in a convertible! And if there's rain in the forecast, you'd better plan on staying in! Of course, once you sleep on that hair, it reverts to bed-head no matter what you might do. So the next day, you have to start all over again. You have to reset the hair.

The same is true with setting your heart. You can't expect to set your heart one time and have it last for months on end. Give things a day or two and you're looking at proverbial bed-head. We need to continually set our hearts on God's Word. We need to daily set our heart and soul to seek God. We need to set and reset.

6. Setting our hearts requires conviction, determination, and some good old-fashioned stick-to-itiveness. Repetition is also a good thing. How did Paul encourage Timothy to stay on the right track? The admonition was important enough to repeat it in two of his letters —1 Timothy 6:11 and 2 Timothy 2:22.

7. Have you ever considered that there are role models in Scripture for heart-setting? Check out what the angel said to one of our favorite prophets in Daniel 10:12.

8. Let's take a quick peek at one of those Deuteronomy passages again. Fill in the two key words.

"For if you _____ _____ all these commandments which I command you to do . . . " —Deuteronomy 11:22 NKJV

9. Setting your heart, setting your affections, setting your mind — it all means keeping on with what is right. What does Jude 1:21 tell us about keeping ourselves?

DIGGING DEEPER

Setting our hearts is something we will do with great frequency for the rest of our lives here on earth. We're in this for the long haul! What does the psalmist compare such a setting to in Psalm 84:5? Why is this comparison apt?

PONDER & PRAY

None of us likes a "bad hair day" any more than we do a "bad heart day." Let your prayers in the week ahead be filled with heart-setting. Ask the Lord to show you what preparations you need to make in your own heart for the journey ahead of you. Pray for stick-to-itiveness and endurance for the storms ahead, which often make our resolve go limp. God will honor our efforts and give us the strength we need to live as we should.

TRINKET TO TREASURE

Your trinket for the week could be nothing else but a curler. Keep it handy, and every time you look at it, you can remember that more than your hair needs setting. Our affections must be set on things above. Our hearts must be set to understand the Word. We need to set our hearts to seek the Lord. If you don't take the time to set everything properly, you will find yourself having a "bad hair day" in your heart.

✦ NOTES & PRAYER REQUESTS ✦

_____

_____

_____

_____

_____

_____

_____

CHAPTER 8

LOVE IS KIND

"I KNOW THAT YOU ARE A GRACIOUS AND MERCIFUL GOD,
SLOW TO ANGER AND ABUNDANT IN LOVINGKINDNESS."

Jonah 4:2 NKJV

When we travel long distances and cannot get home before day's end, we must seek out alternative places to rest. For this very purpose, various hotels and motels have cropped up all over the country. When we check into a hotel, we pay for a room in which we can sleep. The accommodations are simple, but they meet our basic needs—bed and bathroom, pillows, blankets and towels. They're nothing fancy, but that hardly matters when the lights are turned out. Many a hotel has found creative ways to make their guests feel welcome. Though all we pay for is the room, they provide small amenities to make our stay a comfortable one. Tiny bottles of shampoo, bars of soap,

CLEARING
✦ THE ✦
COBWEBS

What is the fanciest hotel you've ever stayed in? What most impressed you about your accommodations?

> *God pours His love over us, and we are changed.*
>
> Nicole Johnson

extra blankets in the closet, a coffee pot, an iron-ing board. Wakeup calls, swimming pools, exer-cise facilities, and shuttle buses. Maid service, room service, shirt laundries, shoe shines. The more expensive the hotel, the more elaborate the services they offer to their guests. Turndown services, monogrammed bathrobes, fruit baskets, and the epitome of luxury—the mint on the pil-low.

Technically speaking, these little kindnesses were not required. All we really needed was a bed for the night. But the hotel staff went beyond what was expected of them in order to make us feel special. God's kindness is a little like this. We need His love, and His love would be enough for us. But God embellishes His love with kindness. God's love is kind, and His kindness makes His love all the more welcome.

1. What does Psalm 117:2 say about God's kindness?

2. God's love and His kindness are so intertwined, that the Scriptures put the two words together—lovingkindness. Match the verses below:

___ Nehemiah 9:17	a. Your lovingkindness and Your truth preserve me.
___ Psalm 42:8	b. The LORD your God is greatly kind.
___ Psalm 40:11	c. "With everlasting kindness I will have mercy."
___ Psalm 69:16	d. You are God, abundant in kindness.
___ Psalm 119:76	e. "My kindness shall not depart from you."
___ Isaiah 54:8	f. Your lovingkindness is good.
___ Isaiah 54:10	g. The LORD reigns with lovingkindness all day long.
___ Joel 2:13	h. Let Your merciful kindness be my comfort.

3. God's kindness extends to all people, even to those who are not grateful for it! This kindness is one way in which God draws us to Himself, leading us to repentance. What was the ultimate kindness of God, according to Titus 3:4?

Now is the time to live as Christ lived. Now is the time to love as Christ loved.

Sheila Walsh

> *God loves you . . . and*
> *that changes everything.*
>
> Nicole Johnson

4. Paul spoke of God's kindness. According to Ephesians 2:7, what did Paul compare God's kindness to us through Christ Jesus to?

We live in a day and age where kindness is optional. It seems to have gone the way of common courtesies. Kindness has fallen into disuse, and it's difficult to define. Oh, it crops up now and again. We tell our children to be kind to animals. Video stores employ small stickers with the pithy plea: "Be kind. Rewind." Bumper stickers urge passersby to commit random acts of kindness. But kindness is more than simple courtesies. Kindness is an attribute of God, which we can both enjoy and reflect.

5. How did David regard the lovingkindness of God, according to Psalm 36:7? And in that same verse, what did this lovingkindness lead people to do?

6. What is the follow-up prayer we find in Psalm 36:10?

Blessing and honor, dominion and power be unto You, Most High God.

Thelma Wells

> *We are safe in the arms of Jesus.*
>
> Barbara Johnson

7. David doesn't stop with gratitude. His praise of God's love and kindness becomes quite effusive! How does Psalm 63:3 describe the lovingkindness of God?

8. Kindness is mentioned alongside love in the most famous biblical dissertation on the subject. What does 1 Corinthians 13:4 tell us about love?

9. Last but not least, kindness is a quality listed among eight other significant ones. Where does Galatians 5:22 say that kindness in our hearts comes from?

DIGGING DEEPER

God has dealt kindly with us, and as we grow to be more like Him, kindness blossoms in our own hearts. What did Paul urge believers to do in Romans 12:10, and how does he describe kind behavior in this verse?

PONDER & PRAY

You can't be kind with nobody around to be kind to! This week pray not only that you'll have eyes opened to see God's kindness to you, but that He'll place people in your path so you can show kindness to them. Acts of kindness needn't be random. Be purposeful in reflecting this attribute of God in the days ahead.

TRINKET TO TREASURE

God could have decided that all of mankind needed "tough love" and kept it at that. Take it or leave it. But He didn't. God infused His love for us with kindness. Since we've compared this to hotels providing more than the barest of necessities for their guests, this week's trinket will be a mint — the famous mint on your pillow. God, like our hotel management, goes above and beyond to make us feel welcome.

✦ NOTES & PRAYER REQUESTS ✦

_____

_____

_____

_____

_____

_____

CHAPTER 9

ABIDING IN LOVE

"AS THE FATHER LOVED ME,
I ALSO HAVE LOVED YOU; ABIDE IN MY LOVE"

John 15:9 NKJV

Every little girl has dreamed at some time about living in a castle. There's something appealing about those sprawling fortresses, with their moats and turrets and drawbridges and ballrooms. For some reason, they sound like perfection. There would be tapestries and chandeliers and beautiful paintings on every wall. There would be maids and a housekeeper and a butler and grooms and a cook. There would be extensive lawns with peacocks strutting across them. There would be formal gardens, reflecting ponds, and bowers of roses. It all sounds so beautiful. But the idea of living in a castle is probably a whole lot more enjoyable than actually living in one. Stone floors would

CLEARING
✦ THE ✦
COBWEBS

What is the largest house you've ever visited?

> *To love as Jesus loves is a tall order for us falliable human beings.*
>
> Marilyn Meberg

be cold underfoot. Wide halls would be drafty. High-ceilinged rooms would be hard to heat. Chinks in the mortar might let in all sorts of critters—ants, spiders, crickets, roaches, snakes, salamanders, mice, rats, bats. Cobwebs in every corner. Musty smells wafting up from the cellars. On rainy days, the whole place becomes as dank as the dungeons, and the hunting hounds lolling by the fireplace give off the distinct odor of wet dog.

Even the most romantic, idealistic homes on this earth have their little imperfections. They can only disappoint us. But believers needn't worry over such things. Our real life is hidden away in Jesus Christ, and we abide in His love.

1. We are loved lavishly. How does Paul describe God's love for us in Romans 5:5?

2. How does Jesus say we are loved in John 15:9? What does He invite us to do?

3. Abiding. It's moving in. It's making yourself comfortable. It's making yourself at home. Scripture tells us that if we belong to God, we have a home with Him.

___ Psalm 91:1	a. Whoever believes in Jesus won't abide in darkness.
___ John 8:31	b. If you keep My commandments, you'll abide in My love.
___ John 8:35	c. Abide in Him while you await His coming.
___ John 12:46	d. We shall abide under the shadow of the Almighty.
___ John 15:9	e. A son abides in his Father's house forever.
___ John 15:10	f. We are invited to abide in Jesus' love.
___ 1 John 2:28	g. If you abide in My word, you are My disciples.

4. Abiding in love gives us the idea of being surrounded by love, of living in love. Paul gives us another picture of this abiding—while we are abiding in Christ, Christ is abiding in us. How does Ephesians 3:17 describe our relationship to love?

5. Rooted, growing, bearing fruit—this picture is used consistently in Scripture for those who abide in Christ and His love.

- According to John 15:4, what must we do in order to bear fruit?

- How do we know that we are abiding in Jesus, according to 1 John 4:13?

- Who abides with us forever, according to John 14:16?

6. We abide in Christ's love. His Spirit abides in us. And by abiding, we bear fruit. What is that fruit, according to Galatians 5:22, 23?

7. We put our trust in God. We abide in Him. How does David describe the attitude of his heart because of this in Psalm 5:11?

> *Faith carries us through life's unknowns and God's mysteries.*
>
> Patsy Clairmont

8. What is another description of the one who loves the Lord, found in Judges 5:31?

9. This invitation of the Lord's for us to come and abide in His love has interesting complexities. Take a careful look at 1 John 4:16—just who is in what?

DIGGING DEEPER

Nothing on this earth can satisfy our longing for heaven. But we can lay up for ourselves treasures in heaven. They'll be waiting for us somewhere where thieves cannot break in and steal, and where moth and rust cannot decay. Take a look at these verses that talk about just those things:

- Matthew 6:19, 20
- Luke 12:32
- John 14:2

PONDER & PRAY

Over the next few days, consider what it means to abide in Christ. We must depend upon Him, draw our strength from Him, feel at home with Him. Pray that your roots will continue to go down deep into His love. Pray that you will be able to flourish, grow, and bear fruit.

TRINKET TO TREASURE

There are times that we need to be reminded that we can never be completely happy in this world. Even living in a castle would have its downside. That's why this week's trinket is a little spider—to remind you that even the most elegant mansion on this earth will have cobwebs in the corners. Our true home is with God, and until we join Him, we can abide in His love.

CHAPTER 10

COMMANDED TO LOVE

"BELOVED, IF GOD SO LOVED US, WE OUGHT TO LOVE ONE ANOTHER."

1 John 4:11 NKJV

I can't remember a morning of my growing-up life that didn't smell like coffee. Both of my parents always started their day with a cup or two, so the house was filled with the fragrance of it. I love the smell of coffee! But as a youngster I wasn't allowed to touch the stuff. "It'll stunt your growth," I was warned. "It'll put hair on your chest." And so they put me off. When I got older, and finally got the chance to sample some coffee, I was deeply disappointed. The dark liquid was so hot, it scalded my tongue. It tasted bitter, even when I tried adding creamer. And it left a bad taste in my mouth and a sour feeling in my stomach. That was enough of that! Coffee was an acquired

CLEARING
✦ THE ✦
COBWEBS

Some foods require a more "educated palate" to appreciate. What are some of the more exotic foods you've sampled . . . and liked?

> *I need truth in strong doses like a great cup of coffee in the morning.*
>
> Nicole Johnson

taste, and I didn't care to acquire it. From then on, I'd just not be a coffee drinker.

Coffee shops began popping up everywhere. And more and more of the bookstores I so loved started adding little cafes. There's something cozy about being asked to go out for coffee. I felt as if I was missing out on something. Then, came the fateful trip back home to visit family. You see, my sister was working at a Starbucks® at the time. She thought I should try some of the delights of her profession, and had something called a Mocha Frappuccino® concocted for me. Do you know? If you add enough sugar, chocolate, and whipped cream to coffee, it tastes pretty good!

Now consider this. We are commanded to love people as God loves them, but that's not always easy to do. People can be so disagreeable (bitter and sour), we'd just as soon swear off them for good. They're an acquired taste we'd rather not cultivate. But just as sweeteners make coffee more palatable, love makes the difference in our relationships. When we have the love of God for the people in our lives, they become bearable—even welcome!

1. When Jesus came, He brought a new commandment for those who loved Him. What was it, according to John 13:34?

2. What began as something startling and new became the standard to live by. How does the beloved disciple refer to this commandment of Christ's in 2 John 1:5?

3. Over and over again, we are told that we should love one another. But hang on! Should? That makes it sound as though we have some wiggle room—we *should* love people, but it doesn't always happen. Nope. Love is commanded, and there's no way of getting around that!

1 John 3:23—"And this is His _____: that we should _____ on the _____ of His Son Jesus Christ and _____ _____ _____, as He gave us _____" (NKJV).

1 John 4:7, 11, 12—"_____, let us _____ one another, for _____ is of God; and everyone who _____ is born of God and knows God . . . ._____, if God so _____ us, we also ought to _____ one another . . . .If we _____ one another, God _____ in us, and His _____ has been _____ in us" (NKJV).

1 Timothy 1:5 — "Now the _____ of the _____ is _____ from a _____ _____, from a _____ _____, and from _____ _____" **(NKJV)**.

> *Every good life is a balance of duty and bliss. We will be called upon to do things we would rather not. Sometimes people say, "Just follow your heart," but that isn't necessarily the right approach. We have to weigh decisions by the word of God.*
>
> Barbara Johnson

4. We cannot love God without loving our fellow believers. The two go hand in hand, and we can't have one without the other. In fact, this is commanded. What does 1 John 4:21 have to say about it?

5. If we're to succeed in this acquired taste of brotherly love, what two ingredients are absolutely essential? Paul prays they'll be ours in 2 Thessalonians 3:5.

The child's game of Simon Says is quite popular around our house. Daddy is usually Simon, and he leads a very energetic game. Yes, there's nothing like a good Simon Says workout to tire out the family before bedtime. But is it so easy to play Simon Says with our emotions? How many of us have been told "You're going to eat that . . . and you're going to like it!" We may have choked down our veggies, but did we really like them just because we were commanded to? How can we possibly order our emotions around? The very idea makes us rebel. But stop a minute and think. The heart will often follow where we lead it with our heads. What begins as going through the motions may just surprise you by coming from sincere love in the end.

6. What does Romans 13:8 say that we owe to one another as believers?

> *The human heart is selfish, prefers its own way, fights being molded by God, and doesn't want to give in when we don't get what is "rightfully ours." We're stubborn, prideful, and strong-willed, and these unbecoming characteristics are most starkly revealed in our relationships.*
>
> Luci Swindoll

7. Just as love is a commandment, loving is the fulfillment of the law! Why does Paul say love fulfills the law in Romans 13:10?

8. It's clear enough that we need to love one another, but that brings up the question of "How!?!" How do we even know where to begin? What does Paul tell us in 1 Thessalonians 4:9?

9. What does Paul tell us to put on in Colossians 3:14, and why?

DIGGING DEEPER

Some people are easier to love than others. We just seem to "click" with certain people. There are many reasons for this—personalities, interests, similarities, backgrounds, goals, etc. But that doesn't get us off the hook of loving anybody else. Consider Luke 6:32. How does this affect your understanding of God's command to love others?

If you only love the lovable, do you expect a pat on the back? Run-of-the-mill sinners do that. —Luke 6:32 MSG

PONDER & PRAY

This week, ponder over the people in your life. Who is easy to love, and who makes it a challenge for you? Ask the Lord to teach you how to love as He does. Tell Him of your willingness to obey His command to love one another. Ask for inspiration in finding ways to show God's love to those around you. And when you find those who are difficult to love, ask for special grace to acquire a taste for what may seem distasteful at the outset. The love of God will help to sweeten the duty.

TRINKET TO TREASURE

Love is not so easy at times. There are people out there who leave a bitter taste in our mouths. But an acquired taste for people comes through God's own loving ways. Your trinket for this week is coffee beans. Small and fragrant, they hold the promise of something good. Just as it takes a heavy dose of sugar and whipped cream to make coffee palatable to some of us, we must have God's own love for others if we are to fulfill His commandment to love one another.

✦ NOTES & PRAYER REQUESTS ✦

LOVE COMPELS US

"FOR THE LOVE OF CHRIST COMPELS US . . ."

2 Corinthians 5:14 NKJV

In the King James Version, we are told, "Love constrains us." What does that mean—constrain? Newer translations say, "Love compels us." When we are constrained or compelled to do something, it means that we can't help ourselves. We are motivated to act. We simply *must* do a thing.

There are plenty of examples in life of things people do, almost compulsively. If the phone rings, we drop what we're doing and make a dash to answer it. If there's a catchy tune playing, we tap our feet in time. When we see someone yawn, we cannot help but yawn as well. When we enter the sanctuary of a great cathedral, we are compelled to whisper, if we speak at all.

CLEARING ✦ THE ✦ COBWEBS

Have you ever been pregnant, and had some complete stranger walk up and put their hand on your bulging abdomen, and wondered why they felt compelled to do so?

When we see a penny lying on the ground, we bend over and pick it up. And when someone smiles at us, we smile at them in turn.

In this same way, God's love in our hearts constrains us to act in a certain way. It changes our behavior. It compels us.

1. We often hear Christian liberty played up—"We are free in Christ!"—without any mention of the obligations that such liberty carries. What does Galatians 5:13 say about liberty and the opportunity it brings?

> *Fulfill my joy by being like-minded, having the same love, being of one accord, of one mind.*
> *Philippians 2:2* NKJV

2. What would give Paul great joy, according to Philippians 2:2?

3. What is Paul's prayer for believers in 1 Thessalonians 3:12?

4. Paul uses a unique imagery to describe the lives of believers in Colossians 2:2. What does he say love does for us in this verse?

> *I turn to the Word of God to remind myself who God is and who He longs to be in our lives.*
>
> Patsy Clarimont

5. This same illustration is used in Ephesians 4:16:

The whole _____ (all the believers that make up the Church) _____ and _____ together (intertwined, and united for a purpose)

By what every _____ _____ (each having a special part to play)

According to the _____ _____ (together accomplishing much more)

By which every _____ does its _____ (than we could ever do alone)

Causes _____ of the _____ (both in numbers and in maturity)

For the _____ of itself in _____ (each one strengthened because they know they have a place and they are loved)

> *How do we truly give up our agendas? How do we genuinely say, "not my will but Yours, Lord"?*
>
> Marilyn Meberg

As children, we generally needed help in getting ourselves on to the path of good behavior. Mothers were always prompting us to remember our manners and say the polite thing. We needed strong urging to eat our vegetables and keep our room clean. Teachers had to enforce their assignments with pop quizzes and report cards. All these things compelled us to do the right thing. But even as adults, the right thing doesn't always come easily. As believers, we are compelled to do the right thing by God. He saved our lives, and our gratitude compels us to live for Him. His love for us compels us to love Him in return. We might not have a mother prompting us to remember our P's and Q's, but the Spirit compels us. He nudges us in the right direction.

6. Here is a good rule of thumb from the pen of Paul. What does he desire us to do, according to 1 Corinthians 16:14?

7. Just as we said earlier in this study that we cannot be kind if we do not have someone to be kind to, we cannot be loving with no one to love. Perhaps that's why some of the best verses about love in the Bible have to do with our relationships with other people.

• According to 1 Peter 1:22, when we obey the truth, we do what?

• Sometimes, it just isn't easy to be loving. How does Ephesians 4:2 describe our love then?

• What proverb does Peter quote about loving one another in 1 Peter 4:8?

> *And above all things have fervent love for one another, for love will cover a multitude of sins.*
>
> 1 Peter 4:8 NKJV

> *We might hear a child's laughter or feel a loved one's hand squeezing ours and suddenly feel overwhelmed with the abundant joy God provides us in our ordinary, humdrum lives.*
>
> Barbara Johnson

8. What interesting aspects of love are brought up in Hebrews 10:24?

9. What does Hebrews 13:1 exhort us to do?

DIGGING DEEPER

There are more examples of love and its compelling force in the lives of believers. Here are just a few examples:

- 1 Timothy 4:12 — Our lives can serve as an example of love.
- Titus 2:4 — Love compels our actions within our homes.
- Proverbs 17:9 — Love knows when to forgive and forget.

PONDER & PRAY

This week, ponder over God's plan for His people. Why did He want us to be so knit together? What gets in the way of unity in the Church? Who has God placed in your path that you feel compelled to love? Then pray. Pray for sensitivity to the compelling of the Spirit in your heart. Pray for a love that can bear with the ones you find hard to warm up to. Pray for a love that can cover a multitude of sins. And pray for a love that will last, and continue to compel you into good works for the rest of your life.

TRINKET TO TREASURE

"See a penny, pick it up, all the day you'll have good luck!" Whether we're motivated by that silly little children's rhyme or by the frugality of a penny-pincher, most of us will bend over and pick up a penny in a parking lot. It's one of those things we're just compelled to do. Your trinket this week is a penny, and it can serve to remind you of the other things we're compelled to do. God's love compels us to do things we mightn't have done otherwise. His love compels us to live as loving people.

✦ NOTES & PRAYER REQUESTS ✦

BELOVED

"GOD LOVES YOU DEARLY,
AND HE HAS CALLED YOU TO BE HIS VERY OWN PEOPLE."

Romans 1:7 NLT

hen my husband and I were dating, his nickname for me was Little One. When my daughter got a parakeet for her birthday, she named her Precious. When my son was tiny, we called him Bugaboo. What is it about us that makes us give pet names to the things we love? They're nicknames. They're terms of endearment. Some are familiar—honey, dear, sweetheart. Some are adorable—punkin, peanut, cutie pie. Some we use for our children—kiddo, sonny, princess. Some seem to be regional—honeychild, sugar, boo. Some we give to our grandfathers—poppy, paw paw, gumpy. Some are reserved for our beloved grandmothers—nana, bubby,

CLEARING ✦ THE ✦ COBWEBS

Did your parents have a nickname for you when you were growing up?

> *Fear not, for I have redeemed you; I have called you by your name; you are Mine.*
>
> Isaiah 43:1 NKJV

marmee. Some are sentimental—toots, sweetie, babe. Some seem over-romantic—dear heart, darling, lovie. Some sound downright silly—schnookims, poopse, iddy biddy diddums.

Whatever the name, we bestow them for a reason. They mean something to us, they betoken our feelings, and they stick.

1. There is no doubt that we are precious to God. What does Isaiah 43:1, 4 say about God's love for His people?

2. The life that was traded for ours was that of Jesus. "He paid for you with the precious lifeblood of Christ, the sinless, spotless Lamb of God" (1 Pet. 1:19 NLT). God made it very clear that His Son was precious to Him. In fact, the Father pronounced it three times during Christ's ministry.

Matthew 3:17—"A voice from heaven said, 'This is my _____ _____, and I am _____ _____ with him'" (NLT).

Matthew 12:18 — "Look at my _____, whom I have _____. He is my _____, and I am very _____ with him" (NLT).

Matthew 17:5 — "Even as he said it, a bright cloud came over them, and a voice from the cloud said, 'This is my _____ _____, and I am _____ _____ with him. _____ to him'" (NLT).

3. What does 1 Peter 1:7 say is more precious to God than mere gold?

> *God tells us that He knew us in our mother's womb. He tells us that He knows us, even better than we know ourselves. And best of all, He knows something beyond what we know: He knows what He is calling us to become.*
>
> Nicole Johnson

> *When you look at everyday life as a gift from God and as your gift to Him—and as one little piece of the puzzle of purpose that God has planned for you from the beginning of the universe— then each day can be an exciting occasion for discovering the divine appointments God has for you.*
>
> Thelma Wells

4. What else is precious to God, according to 1 Peter 3:4?

*I*n a more Victorian time, there were certain accepted ways of telling a girl what your feelings for her were. And there were equally stringent ways in which a gal could respond appropriately. For instance, back then, men could say it with flowers. A lot of thought went into the flowers they sent to their chosen lady, because each sprig and twig had special significance. Asters for daintiness, buttercups for cheerfulness, yellow roses for friendship, violets for modesty, camellias for admiration, daffodils for respect, geranium for preference, gladiolus for love at first sight, and sweetpeas for good-bye. A red carnation said, "My heart aches for you." A gardenia said, "You're lovely." A primrose said, "I can't live without you."

When a girl received a posy from a gentleman, she could read the message he sent in the flowers, and decide how to respond. If she didn't care much for the fellow, she'd just plunk the bunch in a bowl of water and be done with it. However, if she wanted to let the man know her feelings were mutual, she'd choose a few blooms from the bouquet and fix them in her hair or pin them to her blouse. When he saw her flowers there, he knew she returned his feelings. And often, when they married, she would carry those same flowers in her bridal bouquet.

God doesn't need flowers to send His message of love to us, though He made them all. But we can respond to Him by taking the time to grace our lives and crown ourselves with the gifts He bestows. He has loved us, do we love Him? He has poured out His love into our lives, do we share it with others?

5. We are dear to God. What does Romans 1:7 tell us about God's love for us?

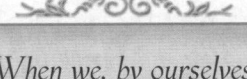

When we, by ourselves, know who we are in Christ, when we have a strong personal relationship with Him, then we have so much to offer each other.

Sheila Walsh

6. Even Jesus had a pet name of sorts for His Heavenly Father. Jesus called God, "Abba," which was much like our own word, "Daddy." What does God call us in Ephesians 5:1?

> *Therefore be imitators of God as dear children.*
>
> Ephesians 5:1 NKJV

7. God calls us His beloved. We are close to His heart, cherished and precious. David called upon God for rescue in Psalm 60:5. Why is he so sure that the Lord will respond?

8. We are all called dear, precious, and beloved of God. But He goes a step further. In a way, He gives us each a pet name. What does Revelation 2:17 promise we shall receive from the Lord?

> *The human heart quests for satisfaction and keeps at it until it finds some kind of peace in God.*
>
> Luci Swindoll

9. The theme verse from the beginning of this study was from Jeremiah.

> *I've never quit loving you and never will. Expect love, love, and more love!* — Jeremiah 31:3 MSG

Is there anything else you could possibly need to convince you of the truth of this?

DIGGING DEEPER

Many commentaries say that the Song of Solomon gives a picture of God's love for His people and Christ's love for the church. When's the last time you perused this racy bit of ancient poetry? Read through it this week, and make a note of all the times you'll see "beloved" used!

PONDER & PRAY

This week, ponder over the various lessons on love you've responded to most strongly. Pray for a greater grasp on just how much God cares about you. Revel in the fact that you are beloved of God. Then ask God for ways in which you can respond to His love. What would He have you do with this abundance that is yours?

TRINKET TO TREASURE

Your last trinket for this study series is a lovely bouquet. God loves you deeply, richly, fully. You are His chosen one, His beloved, His waiting bride. What message do you find in the flowers He has given to you? What message would you send to Him in the way you use those flowers to crown your head and heart? Respond to His love with your whole heart. Bask in it. Trust in it. Depend on it. Receive it!

SHALL WE REVIEW?

Every chapter has added a new trinket to your treasure trove of memories. Let's remind ourselves of the lessons they hold for us!

1. A doughnut.

Doughnuts are delicious, but there's nothing like a hot, fresh doughnut right from the source. God is love, and He is the source of love. Deep as it is, our own love has its limits, but God's love is perfect, limitless, unparalleled.

2. A key.

Because of His so great love for us, God sent Jesus to set us free. He's rescued us from the slavery of sin, unlocked the bars to our heart, and opened up a whole new world to us.

3. A piglet.

The runt of the litter, to be exact—to remind us of the joy of being chosen, and that God chose us, not because we were so very desirable, but because we needed Him.

4. A daisy.

We don't need to wonder if God loves us, plucking at petals as we say, "He loves me, He loves me not." We know He loves us because He's told us so.

5. A mirror.

The love in our heart is a reflection of the love God has for us. Our heart responds to the heart of God.

6. A plant mister.

There are practical consequences to loving the Lord. Our love for God, in order for it to mature, must be accompanied by obedience.

7. A curler.

More than our hair needs setting. Our affections must be set on things above. Our hearts must be set to understand the Word. We need to set our hearts to seek the Lord.

8. A mint on the pillow.

God infused His love for us with kindness. Like a hotel's token of comfort, God's kindness toward us goes above and beyond to make us feel welcome.

9. A spider.

Even the most elegant mansion on this earth will have cobwebs in the corners. Our true home is with God, and until we join Him, we can abide in His love.

10. Coffee beans.

Just as coffee is an acquired taste, people can take some getting used to. The love of God helps us to fulfill His commandment to love one another.

11. A penny.

Just as we feel compelled to bend down and pick up a penny off the ground, God's love compels us to live as loving people.

12. A bouquet.

We are God's chosen ones, His beloved, His waiting bride. We have God's love. Bask in it. Trust in it. Depend on it. Receive it!

WHAT SHALL WE STUDY NEXT?

Women of Faith® has a series of study guides on various topics to help you draw closer to God.

KNOWING GOD'S WORD

For many people, the thought of studying brings back unpleasant memories of school. Those were the days when we were told what we needed to know. We endured lectures, library-time, projects, and pop quizzes. Homework was the scourge of our young lives—dull, daily, and always due. We only learned what we needed to know for the test. We retained our knowledge just long enough to secure a passing grade, then promptly forgot it all. None of us really expected to need to know algebra outside of high school. And when we finally scraped our way through our senior year and across the graduation platform, we were determined never to open another textbook again.

Of course that's not everyone's experience. But still, most people retain the notion that learning takes place in the classroom, and when you're through with school, you're through with "book learning." And of course, that's not really the case. We can and do learn, and we needn't enroll in a class to do it. With a basic understanding of the tools

we need and a willingness to apply ourselves to our studies, we can enjoy a lifetime of learning.

This Bible study has a two-fold purpose. First, it is designed to teach you how to study the Scriptures. It introduces you to the tools and techniques you need to know. And secondly, while we're learning how to study the Bible, we'll be learning all about what the Bible tells us about itself. This will give us a hands-on approach. We'll be learning something while we learn how to learn! Interested? I think this is going to be fun. Let's go!

LIVING A LIFE OF BALANCE

Mobiles. Whether constructed from pipe cleaners and yarn, or copper tubing and glass balls, they're pieces of art. A mobile is a pretty affair, strung together with care, its parts in tenuous equilibrium, and hung where it can be gently moved by passing air currents. It suspends from a single point, but gradually fans out to include a complex array of items, each poised upon its own thread. The secret to a good mobile is balance. Each piece is placed in careful conjunction to the others, so that they offset each other. They hang in a pretty symmetry, delicately balanced. If you were to take away just one bauble from this painstaking arrangement, the whole mobile would hang askew. Balance would be lost. And if you tried to add something new to the array, it would wobble off kilter. Balance would be lost again.

So many of us yearn for balance in our lives. We hope to find that precise alignment which will leave all our daily responsibilities in perfect harmony. But as believers we seem to have so many more ways to be thrown awry. We aren't just balancing our household schedules with work, diet, rest, and exercise. No ma'am! That might take care of physical balance. But we must also consider the spiritual balance of our lives. What is the state of our heart? How are we handling the tenuous balance between faith and sight, between love and obedience, between longing and contentment?

This study doesn't come with a pocket organizer and promotional video — *12 Lessons to a Better, More Balanced You!* But it starts at the heart of things. We can hardly expect our physical routine to give us the balanced lifestyle we long for if our heart is out of kilter. Why not start within, and allow the Lord to work through the intricacies until we can find the equilibrium we need?

GIVING GOD YOUR ALL

Are you familiar with the story, *The Emperor's New Clothes*? Two cunning con artists are able to take in an entire nation because nobody wants to look foolish. You see, they set themselves up as master tailors, and offer to create a new suit of clothes for the emperor. The emperor, being a trifle vain, is enormously pleased at the prospect of new finery . . . until the first fitting. With a knowing gleam in their eyes, the conniving tailors display their handiwork, made from a most remarkable fabric. This cloth is so fine, so rare, so miraculously wrought that only the best of men can see it. Those who are unable to see it are fools, unworthy of the position they hold. The emperor is stunned! He'd never considered himself a fool, but for the life of him he cannot see a thing in the tailor's hands. And so he pretends he can see what the others claim to hold. So do all his friends and associates, for no one wants to seem a fool. The suit of clothes is completed, and though they're a bit drafty to the emperor's way of thinking, he agrees to parade through the land, showing them off. But in the end, the truth comes out. There was no cloth. There were no clothes. Everyone has been pretending to see what was not there to begin with, rather than stand out as the only one who could not see.

Have you ever had a secret suspicion that you're missing out on something important in your Christian walk? This believer or that believer will talk about their walk of faith with words like *vibrant*, *intimate*, and *personal*. Their glowing description of their relationship with the divine makes you wonder if you're doing something wrong. Oh, you have faith. You do love God. But to call your dealings with the Lord *vibrant* would be going a little too far. You're not sure what you expected, but you know it wasn't this. But who wants to look foolish? If everyone else says their Christian life is so intimate and personal, ours had better be, too. So we all use the same words. We all nod with understanding when a friend shares about God's working in their hearts. But we wonder why God seems more an acquaintance than a friend to us.

Nobody wants to be labeled a "nominal" Christian. But what changes a life of nodding acquaintance to one of personal intimacy? In a word—surrender. Once we're willing to let God be God, to look to Him in every situation, to value His opinions over any others, to trust Him in every circumstance, and to do what He would have us to do—then the relationship we long for deepens, strengthens, and positively vibrates with vibrancy!

Do you trust God enough to let Him take the reigns? This study takes a look at what the Bible says about yielding to God, giving Him your all, and being able to say, "Not my will, but Thine be done."

LEADER'S GUIDE

Chapter 1

1. "The God of love and peace will be with you" (2 Cor. 13:11 NKJV). We know that God is a loving God, and that God loves us. It doesn't surprise us that Paul would call Him the God of Love.

2. "He who does not love does not know God, for God is love" (1 John 4:8 NKJV). God isn't just the God of love. He's not just a loving God. God *is* love. He's synonymous with love. If we want to know what love is like, we need only look at God, and it all becomes clear!

3. "Your unfailing love is as high as the heavens. Your faithfulness reaches to the clouds" (Ps. 57:10 NLT). Trying to comprehend the measure of God's love is like trying to reach up and touch the sky. It's beyond our capabilities. "Your unfailing love is better to me than life itself; how I praise you" (Ps. 63:3 NLT). A life without God's love is no life at all. "Your unfailing love is higher than the heavens. Your faithfulness reaches to the clouds" (Ps. 108:4 NLT). Okay, I know this sounds like the first one, but it says "higher than the heavens." So instead of reaching for the sky, this would be like touching the stars!

4. c, f, a, g, b, d, e

5. What a comfort to know that God's love isn't stingy. He doesn't hold back, or put conditions on His love. His love is consistent, steady, and utterly faithful. God's love is truly amazing! [You could duplicate the checklist in the Leader's Guide, leaving short-lived, temperamental, stingy, inconsistent, and easy-come, easy-go unchecked.]

6. "May you have the power to understand, as all God's people should, how wide, how long, how high, and how deep his love really is" (Eph. 3:18 NLT). Even if we should begin to grasp how great God's love for us is, we'd just be scraping the surface. Still, we should try to understand. All God's people should know with confidence that they are loved.

7. "The Lord appeared of old to me, saying: 'Yes I have loved you with an everlasting love; Therefore with lovingkindness I have drawn you'" (Jer. 31:3 NKJV). God's love is never-ending, everlasting, eternal. But He doesn't overwhelm us with the sheer vastness of that love. The Lord is gentle with us. He balances His love with kindness, and gently draws our heart to His.

8. "I drew them with gentle cords, with bands of love, and I was to them as those who take the yoke from their neck, I stooped and fed them" (Hos. 11:4 NKJV).

Chapter 2

1. "God **demonstrates** His own **love** toward **us**, in that while we were still **sinners**, Christ **died** for us" (Rom. 5:8 NKJV). God didn't wait for us to prove ourselves. He didn't wait to see how we would turn out. He didn't hold back, hoping that we would become more lovable before He made His choice. He loved us from the start, and was willing to demonstrate that love without a guarantee that we'd respond.

2. "God, who is rich in mercy, because of His great love with which He loved us, even when we were dead in trespasses, made us alive together with Christ (by grace you have been saved), and raised us up together, and made us sit together in the heavenly places in Christ Jesus, that in the ages to come He might show the exceeding riches of His grace in His kindness toward us in Christ Jesus" (Eph. 2:4–7 NKJV). Wow! There's a lot going on in that sentence, but let's focus in on the very first part. Why does God do all this for us? "Because of His great love with which He loved us."

3. "In this the love of God was manifested toward us, that God has sent His only begotten Son into the world, that we might live through Him. In this is love, not that we loved God, but that He loved us and sent His Son to be the propitiation for our sins" (1 John 4:9, 10 NKJV). Each of the two things we're looking at here begin with "in this." In other words, "this is how I showed you I love you." In verse 9, God showed us love by sending Jesus into the world. He was making a way for us to have life—eternal life. In verse 10, God showed us love before we loved Him. He provided for our greatest need before we knew we had it.

4. "Greater love has no one than this, than to lay down one's life for his friends" (John 15:13 NKJV). To sacrifice all for the sake of a friend. To be willing to set aside our own life for the good of another. To die so that they might live.

5. "We know what real love is because Christ gave up his life for us" (1 John 3:16 NLT). Jesus modeled real love. He demonstrated God's love, and the disciples experienced it firsthand. And now they're the ones who describe it to us in Scripture, so that we can know it, too.

6. Comparing different translations of a Scripture verse can be a very good way of shedding new light on a passage. Even the most familiar of verses can hold new insights when we see them in a different way.

7. "Jesus Christ, the faithful witness, the firstborn from the dead, and the ruler over the kings of the earth. To Him who loved us and washed us from our sins in His own blood" (Rev. 1:5 NKJV). Jesus loved us, and His blood was shed to wash our sins away.

8. "He has delivered us from the power of darkness and conveyed us into the kingdom of the Son of His love" (Col. 1:13 NKJV). Wow! Not only are we rescued from the power of darkness, we're transported into a new kingdom. The kingdom of the Son of God's love—that's our new home.

9. "Now may our Lord Jesus Christ Himself, and our God and Father, who has loved us and given us everlasting consolation and good hope by grace" (2 Thess. 2:16 NKJV). Everlasting consolation. Good hope. Let's take a look at that verse in another translation: "May Jesus himself and God our Father, who reached out in love and surprised you with gifts of unending help and confidence" (MSG). God has loved us, and in that love we find the hope we need as we await His return.

Chapter 3

1. "Blessed is the man You choose, and cause to approach You, that he may dwell in Your courts" (Ps. 65:4 NKJV). The Message reads, "Blessed are the chosen! Blessed the guest at home in your place! We expect our fill of good things in your house, your heavenly manse." We are the chosen, and can look for good things from God's hand. And another version says, "What joy for those you choose to bring near, those who live in your holy courts. What joys await us inside your holy Temple" (NLT). God chose us to bring us near to Him.

2. "The LORD did not **set** His **love** on you nor **choose** you because you were more in **number** than any other people, for you were the **least** of all peoples" (Deut. 7:7 NKJV). "The LORD **delighted** only in your fathers, to **love** them; and He **chose** their **descendants** after them, you **above** all peoples" (Deut. 10:15 NKJV).

3. f, d, a, j, b, c, e, i, h, g

4. "Blessed is the nation whose God is the LORD, the people He has chosen as His own inheritance" (Ps. 33:12 NKJV). God's people will be blessed. The chosen ones are blessed. Those God has claimed for His own are blessed.

5. "Just as He chose us in Him before the foundation of the world, that we should be holy and without blame before Him in love" (Eph. 1:4 NKJV). God made His covenant with Abram, and chose his descendants to be His own people. But before Abram became Abraham and Israel became God's children, before the very foundations of the world were established, God chose us! He chose you!

6. "You are a chosen generation, a royal priesthood, a holy nation, His own special people, that you may proclaim the praises of Him who called you out of darkness into His marvelous light" (1 Pet. 2:9 NKJV). God says we are a chosen generation. We are a royal priesthood. We are a holy nation. We are His own special people. And as such what do we do? We proclaim the praises of the One who made us what we are!

7. "God has chosen the foolish things of the world to put to shame the wise, and God has chosen the weak things of the world to put to shame the things which are mighty" (1 Cor. 1:27 NKJV). We may not always feel like it, but we are exactly who God says we are. If He says we're a chosen generation and a royal priesthood, don't argue! But God also knows that we are weak and foolish. Guess we're runts, too! And He's chosen us to put the wise and the mighty to shame. In spite of our imperfections, He will gain glory.

8. "He is a chosen vessel of Mine to bear My name before Gentiles, kings, and the children of Israel" (Acts 9:15 NKJV). "The God of our fathers has chosen you that you should know His will, and see the Just One, and hear the voice of His mouth" (Acts 22:14 NKJV).

9. "He is Lord of lords and King of kings; and those who are with Him are called, chosen, faithful" (Rev. 17:14 NKJV). Isn't it nice to think that we'll be among those who will be known as His—the called, the chosen, the faithful.

Chapter 4

1. "Love one another as I have loved you" (John 13:34 NKJV). "Overwhelming victory is ours through Christ, who loved us" (Rom. 8:37 NLT). "All praise to him who loves us" (Rev. 1:5 NLT). We may not be able to find the whole text of "Jesus Loves Me" in the pages of Scripture, but Jesus' love for us is evident. He loved us enough to come and die, and He loves us still.

2. "For now we see in a mirror, dimly, but then face to face. Now I know in part, but then I shall know just as I am known" (1 Cor. 13:12 NKJV). We may not know it all, but we know all we need to know. And one of the things we can be confident of is God's love for us.

3. e, c, h, a, d, g, b, f

4. "I am not ashamed, for I know whom I have believed and am persuaded that He is able to keep what I have committed to Him until that Day" (2 Tim. 1:12 NKJV). Paul didn't have a shadow of doubt about Jesus' love and power.

5. "We are confident, yes, well pleased rather to be absent from the body and to be present with the Lord" (2 Cor. 5:8 NKJV). Paul was so sure of Jesus' love and power that even death held no fear for him. Paul knew that when he died, he'd be reunited with the Lord who loved him.

6. "Being confident of this very thing, that He who has begun a good work in you will complete it until the day of Jesus Christ" (Phil. 1:6 NKJV). God loves us, and He keeps His promises to us. One of those promises is to finish the work He's begun in our lives.

7. "To know the love of Christ which passes knowledge" (Eph. 3:19 NKJV). Or to use another translation, "May you experience the love of Christ, though it is so great you will never fully understand it" (NLT). Paul says he wants for us to know the love of Christ, but also that Christ's love passes knowledge. It's beyond our comprehension. So what he's saying is that he wants us to know the unknowable! Now that's a paradox!

8. In Romans 8:38, Paul says that he is "persuaded" that Christ's love for him is real and that nothing can stop it. Jesus' love may be beyond our comprehension, but its existence is undeniable. Our hearts are drawn gently to God, even as our minds are persuaded by the evidence of His unshakeable love.

9. "Walk in love, as Christ also has loved us and given Himself for us, an offering and a sacrifice to God for a sweet-smelling aroma" (Eph. 5:2 NKJV). Wherever we go in this world, we can know that we're in the love of Christ. We walk in His love. *The Message* reads this way: "Mostly what God does is love you. Keep company with him and learn a life of love. Observe how Christ loved us. His love was not cautious but extravagant. He didn't love in order to get something from us but to give everything of himself to us. Love like that."

Chapter 5

1. "We know how much God loves us, and we have put our trust in Him" (1 John 4:16 NKJV). Love and trust are closely entwined. God loves us, and we trust Him. How could we not love Him back?

2. "We **love Him** because He **first loved** us" (1 John 4:19 NKJV). That's about as straightforward as you can get!

3. "Choose to love the Lord your God and to obey him and commit yourself to him, for he is your life" (Deut. 30:20 NLT). There are those who choose to respond to God's love and those who do not. We are those who believe Him, trust Him, obey Him—love Him.

4. "I will love You, O LORD, my strength" (Ps. 18:1 NKJV).

5. Our love must be wholehearted. "You shall love the LORD your God with all your heart, with all your soul, with all your strength, and with all your mind" (Luke 10:27 NKJV). Joshua goes on to describe what wholehearted devotion looks like. "To love the LORD your God, to walk in all His ways, to keep His commandments, to hold fast to Him, and to serve Him with all your heart and with all your soul" (Josh. 22:5 NKJV).

6. "Oh, that my actions would consistently reflect your principles!" (Ps. 119:5 NLT). That should be the prayer of all our hearts! "As for you, promote the kind of living that reflects right teaching" (Titus 2:1 NLT). Paul wanted Titus to be a role model, a living example, an object lesson of right living. "You yourself must be an example to them by doing good deeds of every kind. Let everything you do reflect the integrity and seriousness of your teaching" (Titus 2:7 NLT).

7. "And all of us have had that veil removed so that we can be mirrors that brightly reflect the glory of the Lord. And as the Spirit of the Lord works within us, we become more and more like him and reflect his glory even more" (2 Cor. 3:18 NLT). Our lives are like mirrors, reflecting the glory of the Lord.

8. "If anyone loves God, this one is known by Him" (1 Cor. 8:3 NKJV). Or to put it another way, "God has no doubts about who loves him" (CEV). And it is always interesting to see how *The Amplified Bible* expands on things. "But if one loves God truly [with affectionate reverence, prompt obedience, and grateful recognition of His blessing], he is known by God [recognized as worthy of His intimacy and love, and he is owned by Him]" (AMP).

9. "Whom having not seen, you love. Though now you do not see Him, yet believing, you rejoice with joy inexpressible and full of glory" (1 Pet. 1:8 NKJV). We love One we have never seen! This reminds me of Jesus' words to Thomas: "Jesus said to him, 'Thomas, because you have seen Me, you have believed. Blessed are those who have not seen and yet have believed'" (John 20:29 NKJV). Faith is needed for believing, and faith is needed for loving.

Chapter 6

1. "This is love, that we walk according to His commandments. This is the commandment, that as you have heard from the beginning, you should walk in it" (2 John 1:6 NKJV). Throughout all the books John wrote (the Gospel of John, 1, 2, 3 John and Revelation), he's quite adamant that loving God means obeying God. If you love Him, do as He asks.

2. "What does the LORD **require** of you, but to **fear** the LORD your God, to **walk** in all His **ways** and to **love** Him, to **serve** the LORD your God with all your **heart** and with all your **soul**" (Deut. 10:12 NKJV). "Therefore you shall **love** the LORD your God, and **keep** His **charge**, His **statutes**, His **judgments**, and His **commandments** always" (Deut. 11:1 NKJV). "**Earnestly obey** My commandments which I command you today, to **love** the LORD your God and **serve** Him with all your **heart** and with all your **soul**" (Deut. 11:13 NKJV).

3. "My little children, let us not love in word or in tongue, but in deed and in truth" (1 John 3:18 NKJV). We can be very good at putting up a front and pretending to be something we are not. But John gently reminds believers (don't you love how he calls them his little children?) that love cannot be merely lip service. Love in truth is tangible, practical, observable. Love shows itself in deeds.

4. "'He who has My commandments and keeps them, it is he who loves Me. And he who loves Me will be loved by My Father, and I will love him and manifest Myself to him.' Judas (not Iscariot) said to Him, 'Lord, how is it that You will manifest Yourself to us, and not to the world?' Jesus answered and said to him, 'If anyone loves Me, he will keep My word; and My Father will love him, and We will come to him and make Our home with him'" (John 14:21–23 NKJV). Jesus tells His disciples that those who love Him will keep His commandments. Not only that, they'll *have* His commandments (how can you keep what you don't know!). The promise in verse 23 is that "We will come to him and make Our home with Him." God lives in the hearts of those who are His.

5. "By this we know that we love the children of God, when we love God and keep His commandments. For this is the love of God, that we keep His commandments. And His commandments are not burdensome" (1 John 5:2, 3 NKJV). Burdensome (NKJV), troublesome (MSG), irksome, oppressive, and grievous (AMP), difficult (NLT), hard to follow (CEV), too hard (NCV). We needn't feel put upon or oppressed by God's commandments. Remember what Jesus said in Matthew 11:30, "My yoke is easy and My burden is light" (NKJV). There's really no way to get out of obeying God. The yoke may be easy, but it's still a yoke.

6. "Therefore show to them, and before the churches, the proof of your love and of our boasting on your behalf" (2 Cor. 8:24 NKJV). Paul wanted the lives of believers to serve as evidence to what was in their hearts. "You say you love God? Fine! Prove it." Our lives should be the proof of our love.

7. "Blessed is the man who endures temptation; for when he has been approved, he will receive the crown of life which the Lord has promised to those who love Him" (James 1:12 NKJV). Obedience often means resisting temptation and enduring hardship. But the Lord encourages us to hang onto love and hang in there. The rewards will be worth it all.

8. "I have been **crucified** with Christ; it is **no longer** I who **live**, but Christ **lives** in me; and the **life** which I now **live** in the **flesh** I live by **faith** in the Son of God, who **loved** me and **gave** Himself for me" (Gal. 2:20 NKJV).

Chapter 7

1. "And may not be like their fathers, A **stubborn** and **rebellious** generation, A generation that did not **set** its **heart aright**, And whose **spirit** was not **faithful** to God" (Ps. 78:8 NKJV).

2. "How long, you simple ones, will you love simplicity? For scorners delight in their scorning, and fools hate knowledge" (Prov. 1:22 NKJV). "They come to you as people do, they sit before you as My people, and they hear your words, but they do not do them; for with their mouth they show much love, but their hearts pursue their own gain" (Ezek. 33:31 NKJV). "And when you pray, you shall not be like the hypocrites. For they love to pray standing in the synagogues and on the corners of the streets, that they may be seen by men" (Matt. 6:5 NKJV). "Beware of the scribes, who desire to go around in long robes, and love greetings in the marketplaces" (Mark 12:38 NKJV). "Let love be without hypocrisy" (Rom. 12:9 NKJV).

3. j, h, d, f, l, b, e, k, a, g, m, c, i

4. "Set your hearts on all the words which I testify among you today, which you shall command your children to be careful to observe—all the words of this law" (Deut. 32:46 NKJV). Setting your heart on the right things really must begin with the Scriptures. It's where we find out about God and His great love for us, among other things.

5. "Now set your heart and your soul to seek the LORD your God" (1 Chr. 22:19 NKJV). We all want to receive God's love. We all want to set our hearts on the right things. We all want to seek the Lord. But far too often we're too busy with other things. Too many other things are vying for your attention. Don't let them distract you from setting your heart aright.

6. "But you, O man of God, flee these things and pursue righteousness, godliness, faith, love, patience, gentleness . . . " (1 Tim. 6:11 NKJV). "Flee also youthful lusts; but pursue righteousness, faith, love, peace with those who call on the Lord out of a pure heart" (2 Tim. 2:22 NKJV).

7. "Then he said to me, 'Do not fear, Daniel, for from the first day that you set your heart to understand, and to humble yourself before your God, your words were heard; and I have come because of your words'" (Dan. 10:12 NKJV). Daniel set his heart. We all know the stories of eating only veggies and of being thrown into the lion's den.

Daniel was faithful to God, even though circumstances were against him. Why? Because he'd set his heart to understand and he'd humbled himself before God.

8. "For if you **carefully keep** all these commandments which I command you to do" (Deut. 11:22 NKJV). There's not a whole lot of difference between setting your heart to do something and carefully keeping something. Both involve determination and perseverance. Thankfully, we have the Spirit's help in these things.

9. "Keep yourselves in the love of God, looking for the mercy of our Lord Jesus Christ unto eternal life" (Jude 1:21 NKJV). That's where we all want to be. Set your heart on it!

Chapter 8

1. "For His merciful kindness is great toward us" (Ps. 117:2 NKJV).

2. d, g, a, f, h, c, e, b

3. "When the kindness and the love of God our Savior toward man appeared . . ." (Titus 3:4 NKJV). Paul is speaking of Jesus here. God's sending His Son on our behalf was the ultimate manifestation of God's kindness towards mankind. Yet another way of wooing us, drawing us back to Himself.

4. "In the ages to come He might show the exceeding riches of His grace in His kindness toward us in Christ Jesus" (Eph. 2:7 NKJV). Other translations word this verse slightly differently. "God can always point to us as examples of the incredible wealth of his favor and kindness toward us" (NLT). "God has us where he wants us . . . to shower grace and kindness upon us" (MSG). Paul compares God's kindness with great riches, and he says these riches are ours!

5. "How precious is Your lovingkindness, O God! Therefore the children of men put their trust under the shadow of Your wings" (Ps. 36:7 NKJV). God's lovingkindness is precious. "How precious is Your steadfast love" (AMP). "How exquisite your love" (MSG). "Your love is a treasure" (CEV). God's lovingkindness is precious to David—not taken for granted, but recognized and appreciated.

6. "Oh, continue Your lovingkindness to those who know You, and Your righteousness to the upright in heart" (Ps. 36:10 NKJV). Keep it up! Keep it coming! Don't stop now! "Oh, continue!" David's prayer shows both his thankfulness for the kindness God has shown and the desire for that kindness to continue gracing his life.

7. "Your lovingkindness is better than life" (Ps. 63:3 NKJV). God's kindness in loving us is better than life itself! In a way, it's how we know we're really living. "In your generous love I am really living at last" (MSG).

8. "Love . . . is kind" (1 Cor. 13:4 NKJV). It is the very nature of love to be kind. Have you infused your love of family and friends with kindness lately?

9. "The fruit of the spirit is love, joy, peace, longsuffering, kindness . . . " (Gal. 5:22 NKJV). Kindness is born in our hearts as a result of the Spirit's working there. It is one of the fruits of a life lived by the Spirit.

Chapter 9

1. "Now hope does not disappoint, because the love of God has been poured out in our hearts by the Holy Spirit who was given to us" (Rom. 5:5 NKJV). Another translation says, "We know how dearly God loves us, because he has given us the Holy Spirit to fill our hearts with His love" (NLT). *The Message* gives us a more down-to-earth picture of God's love: "We can't round up enough containers to hold everything God generously pours into our lives through the Holy Spirit."

2. "As the Father loved Me, I also have loved you; abide in My love" (John 15:9 NKJV). Abide in His love. Move in. Make ourselves at home. Make God's love our safe haven.

3. d, g, e, a, f, b, c

4. "That Christ may dwell in your hearts through faith; that you, being rooted and grounded in love" (Eph. 3:17 NKJV). In this verse, instead of abiding, Paul uses the picture of being rooted and grounded. When we've made a home for us somewhere, we'll often say we've put down roots. We can be at home in God's love and put down roots into it.

5. "Abide in Me, and I in you. As the branch cannot bear fruit of itself, unless it abides in the vine, neither can you, unless you abide in Me" (John 15:4 NKJV). In order to bear fruit, we have to be connected to the vine. In this case, we're talking about Jesus as the Vine, and the fruit is spiritual. "By this we know that we abide in Him, and He in us, because He has given us of His Spirit" (1 John 4:13 NKJV). We know that we abide in Jesus because we have his Holy Spirit within us. "And I will pray the

Father, and He will give you another Helper, that He may abide with you forever" (John 14:16 NKJV). When Jesus returned to heaven, a Helper was sent to dwell with believers—the Holy Spirit.

6. "The fruit of the Spirit is love, joy, peace, longsuffering, kindness, goodness, faithfulness, gentleness, self-control. Against such there is no law" (Gal. 5:22, 23 NKJV). We are probably pretty familiar with this passage, but notice: One of the fruits of the Spirit in our lives is love!

7. "Let all those rejoice who put their trust in You; Let them ever shout for joy, because You defend them; Let those also who love Your name be joyful in you" (Ps. 5:11 NKJV). Joy! Our trust in the Lord is rewarded with joy.

8. "Let those who love Him be like the sun when it comes out in full strength" (Judg. 5:31 NKJV). We shine like the sun because of the love God pours out in our lives. The signs of it in our hearts is unmistakable.

9. "And we have known and believed the love that God has for us. God is love, and he who abides in love abides in God, and God in him" (1 John 4:16 NKJV). One of the most complex and delightful paradoxes in a believer's life. We are in God—"we who live in love live in God." And at the same time, He is in us—"God lives in them." We may never fully understand how this can be true, but we can rest assured that it does. "We know how much God loves us, and we have put our trust in him. God is love, and all who live in love live in God, and God lives in them" (NLT).

Chapter 10

1. "A new commandment I give to you, that you love one another; as I have loved you, that you also love one another" (John 13:34 NKJV). Such a thing was new and rather startling. Sure, there had been a certain loyalty among God's people before this, but here was a love that crossed boundaries. Jew and Gentile, slave and free—love for one another suddenly put the new believers on equal footing.

2. "And now I plead with you, lady, not as though I wrote a new commandment to you, but that which we have had from the beginning: that we love one another" (2 John 1:5 NKJV). What began in the Gospels as a new commandment, by the end of the New Testament became the standard of Christian living. John writes, not to inform, but to remind. Loving one another was not a new commandment, but Jesus' old, familiar, tried and true commandment for Christian conduct.

3. "And this is His **commandment**: that we should **believe** on the **name** of His Son Jesus Christ and **love one another**, as He gave us **commandment** (1 John 3:23 NKJV). "**Beloved**, let us **love** one another, for **love** is of God; and everyone who **loves** is born of God and knows God . . . .**Beloved**, if God so **loved** us, we also ought to **love** one another. If we **love** one another, God **abides** in us, and His **love** has been **perfected** in us" (1 John 4:7, 11, 12 NKJV). "Now the **purpose** of the **commandment** is **love** from a **pure heart**, from a **good conscience**, and from **sincere faith**" (1 Tim. 1:5 NKJV).

4. "And this commandment we have from Him: that he who loves God must love his brother also" (1 John 4:21 NKJV). God never meant for us to be devout hermits. We're made to live in community with other believers.

5. "Now may the Lord direct your hearts into the love of God and into the patience of Christ" (2 Thess. 3:5 NKJV). It only takes a small stretch to make Paul's prayer here fit our lesson. He asks that the Lord direct our hearts into two things—the love of God and the patience of Christ. And when it comes to dealing with people, those are the two things we need the most—love and patience! May we always show love to one another that is like God's great love for us. And may we have great patience with those who need our love.

6. "Owe no one anything except to love one another, for he who loves another has fulfilled the law" (Rom. 13:8 NKJV). We owe our love to one another. It is one of the most foundational commands of Christianity, one of the earliest commandments. In fact, Christ said that we would be recognized as His disciples because of the great love we show to one another.

7. "Love does no harm to a neighbor; therefore love is the fulfillment of the law" (Rom. 13:10 NKJV). Or as a couple of other translations put it—"No one who loves others will harm them, so love is all the Law demands" (CEV). "You can't go wrong when you love others" (MSG).

8. "But concerning brotherly love you have no need that I should write to you, for you yourselves are taught by God to love one another" (1 Thess. 4:9 NKJV). We don't need Paul's top ten list of ways to love our sisters in Christ. Paul says that God will teach us what to do. He'll nudge us in the right direction and inspire us with ideas of showing love in big and little ways to those who need it most.

9. "But above all these things put on love, which is the bond of perfection" (Col. 3:14 NKJV). Put on love. That makes it sound like a conscious choice, an effort even. We're urged to put on love, for it's "above" and better than any other thing we could choose. Why? Because it's the bond of perfection! "The greatest of these is love."

Chapter 11

1. "You, brethren, have been called to liberty; only do not use liberty as an opportunity for the flesh, but through love serve one another" (Gal. 5:13 NKJV). Yes, we are free in Christ. Yes, we have liberties. But God did not give them to us so that we could squander them on selfish activities. He's given us a chance to shine. These were given to us as opportunities to do good, to freely choose the right thing. When we take our liberty, and spend it in serving one another through love, God is glorified by our more noble choice.

2. "Fulfill my joy by being like-minded, having the same love, being of one accord, of one mind" (Phil. 2:2 NKJV). Paul often prayed for unity within the church. He longed for the people in each little congregation to be known for their love and unity. Nothing made him happier than finding a church working together in one accord.

3. "And may the Lord make you increase and abound in love to one another and to all, just as we do to you" (1 Thess. 3:12 NKJV). Paul's prayer was that love would increase. He wanted it to abound to all within the church. After all, that's how Jesus said His disciples would be recognized — by their love for one another.

4. "That their hearts may be encouraged, being knit together in love" (Col. 2:2 NKJV). Knitting! When we believers show genuine love for one another, our lives become knit together. Our kindness, generosity, helpfulness and experiences bind us to one another as nothing else can.

5. "The whole **body**, **joined** and **knit** together by what every **joint supplies**, according to the **effective working** by which every **part** does its **share**, causes **growth** of the **body** for the **edifying** of itself in **love**" (Eph. 4:16 NKJV).

6. "Let all that you do be done with love" (1 Cor. 16:14 NKJV). Let love be your motivation for action. If we don't make our plans based on whims, spites or appetites, but let love guide us, we cannot go astray.

7. "Since you have purified your souls in obeying the truth through the Spirit in sincere love of the brethren, love one another fervently with a pure heart" (1 Pet. 1:22 NKJV). Peter urges us to love one another with sincerity and with fervency, without any ulterior motives. "With all lowliness and gentleness, with longsuffering, bearing with one another in love" (Eph. 4:2 NKJV). We all have to admit that sometimes, it's hard to love people. Those are the times that we need to take Paul's words to heart. He says to be gentle, patient, and humble as we bear with one another in love. In other words, for the sake of love, we must be willing to put up with someone else! "And above all things have fervent love for one another, for 'love will cover a multitude of sins'" (1 Pet. 4:8 NKJV). For the sake of love, we can forgive much. We needn't be blind to the faults and failings of others, but we can love and accept them in spite of them.

8. "Let us consider one another in order to stir up love and good works" (Heb. 10:24 NKJV). First of all, the writer of Hebrews says we're to "consider one another." Give some thought to who you want to show God's love to—what are their needs, their likes, their interests. In what way would they receive love? What would encourage them the most? Then we are to "stir up love." The love we show to one another doesn't always just happen. There are times when we need to make a conscious effort to reach out with love and kindness to a friend. And lastly, this verse pairs up the love and the good works that accompany them. Demonstrate your love, ladies! Act on it. Show it, and you'll be an encouragement to everyone around you.

9. "Let brotherly love continue" (Heb. 13:1 NKJV). Don't just show a burst of love to the world, then lose interest and move on to other things. God's love compels us to love one another. Make this love, and the good things that it encompasses, your life's work! Let it constrain you. Let it continue.

Chapter 12

1. "I have called you by your name; You are Mine" (Is. 43:1 NKJV). "Others died that you might live, I traded their lives for yours because you are precious to me. You are honored, and I love you" (Is. 43:4 NLT). We are precious in God's sight. He loves us, and He calls us His own. He calls us by name, redeems us, and bids us not to fear for anything.

2. "A voice from heaven said, 'This is my **beloved Son**, and I am **fully pleased** with him'" (Matt. 3:17 NLT). "Look at my **Servant**, whom I have **chosen**. He is my **Beloved**, and I am very **pleased** with him" (Matt. 12:18 NLT). "Even as he said it, a bright cloud came over them, and a voice from the cloud said, 'This is my **beloved Son**, and I am **fully pleased** with him. **Listen** to him'" (Matt. 17:5 NLT).

3. "These trials are only to test your faith, to show that it is strong and pure. It is being tested as fire tests and purifies gold—and your faith is far more precious to God than mere gold" (1 Pet. 1:7 NLT). God loves us, loves us, loves us, and our faith in Him is precious to Him. He was willing to let go of His precious Son for a time in order to secure it.

4. If you knew something was precious to God, wouldn't you go out of your way to give it to Him? Peter tells us, "You should be known for the beauty that comes from within, the unfading beauty of a gentle and quiet spirit, which is so precious to God" (1 Pet. 3:4 NLT). God is very concerned with the attitudes of a woman's heart, and when we display gentleness within, He is so very pleased.

5. "God loves you dearly, and he has called you to be his very own people" (Rom. 1:7 NLT). God loves us—dearly! We are dear to Him. Because of this, He's chosen us—called us to be His very own.

6. "Follow God's example in everything you do, because you are His dear children" (Eph. 5:1 NKJV). God uses more than one kind of human love to try to help us understand how vast and complex His love for us is. He loves us as a groom loves his bride, and He loves us as a father loves his dear child. We are precious to Him.

7. "That Your beloved may be delivered, save with Your right hand, and hear me" (Ps. 60:5 NKJV). Or as another translation puts it, "Use your strong right arm to save us, and rescue your beloved people" (NLT). Of course God will respond to his cry for help! David is sure because he knows how much God loves him.

8. "To him who overcomes . . . I will give him a white stone, and on the stone a new name written which no one knows except him who receives it" (Rev. 2:17 NKJV). We'll each receive a new name from the hand of the Lord. It'll be special, and no one will know it but us.

9. If you need more convincing, go back through the last several weeks of this study and reread the Scriptures about God's love. Those verses are true, and God cannot lie. You are loved, loved, loved. You can expect nothing less than love, love, and more love. Bask in it. Trust in it. Depend on it. Receive it!

THE COMPLETE WOMEN OF FAITH® STUDY GUIDE SERIES

CONTAGIOUS JOY

RECEIVING GOD'S LOVE

CULTIVATING CONTENTMENT

RECEIVING GOD'S GOODNESS

ADVENTUROUS PRAYER

MANAGING YOUR MOODS

LIVING ABOVE WORRY and STRESS

KNOWING GOD'S WORD

LIVING IN JESUS

EXPERIENCING SPIRITUAL INTIMACY

UNDERSTANDING PURPOSE

A LIFE OF WORSHIP

LIVING A LIFE OF BALANCE

ENCOURAGING ONE ANOTHER

DISCOVERING GOD'S WILL FOR YOUR LIFE

GIVING GOD YOUR ALL

WOMEN OF FAITH®

To find these and other inspirational products visit your local Christian retailer.

www.nelsonimpact.com